Pearlie of Great Price

Pearlie

of

Great Price

*Following a dog
into the presence of God*

by HILARY HART

BOOKS

Winchester, U.K.
New York, U.S.A.

First published by O Books, 2007
O Books is an imprint of John Hunt Publishing Ltd.,
The Bothy, Deershot Lodge, Park Lane, Ropley, Hants, SO24 0BE, UK
office1@o-books.net
www.o-books.net

Distribution in:

UK and Europe
Orca Book Services
orders@orcabookservices.co.uk
Tel: 01202 665432
Fax: 01202 666219 Int. code (44)

USA and Canada
NBN
custserv@nbnbooks.com
Tel: 1 800 462 6420
Fax: 1 800 338 4550

Australia and New Zealand
Brumby Books
sales@brumbybooks.com.au
Tel: 61 3 9761 5535
Fax: 61 3 9761 7095

Far East (offices in Singapore,
Thailand, Hong Kong, Taiwan)
Pansing Distribution Pte Ltd
kemal@pansing.com
Tel: 65 6319 9939
Fax: 65 6462 5761

South Africa
Alternative Books
altbook@peterhyde.co.za
Tel: 021 447 5300
Fax: 021 447 1430

Text copyright Hilary Hart 2007

Design: Jim Weaver

ISBN-13: 978 1 84694 029 3
ISBN-10: 1 84694 029 X

A CIP catalogue record for this book is available from
the British Library.

Printed in the US by Maple Vail

Where is the door to God?
In the sound of a barking dog,
In the ring of a hammer,
In a drop of rain,
In the face of
Everyone
I see.

Hafiz

Table of contents

Introduction

Spiritual awakening is a strange mystery with few rules and even fewer explanations. Can anyone really understand how a flower blooms? Is there a reason why one young bird leaves the nest and another is too weak to fly? Can we predict when or why love scoops us from loneliness and delivers us into the nourishing sweetness of belonging?

And in the telling of blossoms and flying and love, so much can be lost, for spiritual truth lives more in the untold than anywhere else, it seems.

But I have a great teacher, who, when he told me to write a story about my spiritual path, gave me the perfect main character around which to weave the tale. He told me to write about my dog, Pearlie.

At the time, his suggestion appeared far from perfect. Pearlie did not seem spiritual, and I could not imagine a book about her. She was a stubborn, pear-shaped, terrier mutt with few interests other than sleeping. Mostly blind in one of her sad eyes, she seemed to be only half here in this world. Her scraggly white hair was tinged on the ends with black, and sometimes she shimmered like a pearl.

It was not easy writing a book about someone who slept most of the time. But the more I looked to Pearlie, the more I understood that she offered just what I needed to tell a good story. And she offered a way for me to live the story that needed to be told – a story of finding what I had been looking for and becoming who I am.

It has not been an easy path. Being with Pearlie meant giving up spiritual life and waking up in the mysteries of life itself. It meant letting go of my grasp on the eternal, so that the eternal could hide and reveal itself where needed. And it meant leaving many attachments behind, including my attachment to my teacher.

It is said when a disciple meets her teacher, her life begins anew. This is how it was for me. I was thirty-five years old when I found my teacher and the lineage to which I belong. From the moment I saw him, I knew nothing would ever be the same. It was as though the world suddenly revealed itself through rainbows and rainbows of new colors. My love for my teacher grew so quickly it was as though I had been waiting forever to find him; it was so powerful that I was certain it held the key to my love for God.

So I was shocked when, after six years by his side, he suddenly told me to look to Pearlie for realization. He explained that spiritual life is very simple. He said what I was looking for was already with me and had been with me for a very long time, and this was what my dog could show me. Then he sent me away to learn this lesson.

His instruction shattered many of my illusions about the spiritual path, for it was nearly impossible to believe that it was not with him – a great mystic absorbed in the infinite emptiness beyond this world – but with Pearlie – an old, terrier mutt – that the divine waited to be known.

It took a long time to notice Pearlie's secrets. It took effort and failure and grace. But I have come to know that my teacher was right. What I had been searching for has always been present. Beyond my devotion for him and even my drive for spiritual Truth, an ancient energy of peace and wholeness, simplicity and complete belonging slowly revealed itself. Love unfurled from within love, and I felt this secret presence first by my feet, or out in the yard, or lying in the big blue doughnut shaped bed in the living room.

When I brought Pearlie home from the shelter, I had not read the parable of the pearl of great price – the New Testament story of the gem merchant "Who, when he had found one pearl of great price, went and sold all that he had, and bought it." I didn't know about losing everything and gaining the one thing that matters. I had never noticed the luminous pearl of the Self, lighting all creation from the inside out.

If I could, I would go back in time. I would never have believed Pearlie was less beautiful than my teacher. I would never have left her behind in my longing for God. I would have loved her right from the start as I loved her in the end, with a love that includes everything and knows that all life is alive with divinity.

But then there would be no story to tell of the sweetness of loss and the tenderness of new love, limitless as life. There would be no story of Pearlie, my own pearl of great price, who guided me from deserts of hearbreak into the ocean of belonging and left me there, alone, in the shining darkness where all stories begin and end.

1

A pearl of great price

The Kingdom of Heaven is like unto a merchant man, seeking goodly pearls: Who, when he had found the pearl of great price, went and sold all that he had, and bought it.

Matthew 13:45

Pearlie

Pearlie did not look like she had come from the streets of Denver, as the shelter worker had warned me, she looked like she just had emerged from a magical thicket in a fairy tale. She entered the adoption room in a cloud of whiteness, large and slow moving, with soft scraggly hair sticking straight out from her face and all around in tangles and tufts. Her giant triangular ears pointed outward, trailing long strands of hair, like wings trailing light.

The shelter worker brought Pearlie to me after I had visited with a smart, light brown Australian shepherd puppy who tempted me with his alert willingness to please. In contrast, Pearlie did not seem interested in pleasing me at all. She had not been treated well by her previous owners, and this was evident in her shy confusion. But she seemed like an angel, with wide-open eyes looking far away. I liked how calm she was. Perhaps she was funny looking with her scraggly fur and big ears, but really, I thought she was beautiful.

After I declared that I would adopt Pearlie, whom they had clearly misnamed "Babette" due to a suggestion of French Briard heritage, we got up to leave the room. But Pearlie wouldn't go anywhere. I tried to assure her she was coming home with me, but maybe she didn't care because she still dug her heels into the floor. Luckily the floor was plastic tile, so I could push from behind as the shelter worker pulled her to the check-out counter. Not until she smelled the fresh air outside the building did she lift her eyes to the world and walk willingly away with me.

Pearlie was three years old and not adventurous. She weighed over sixty-five pounds and was full figured. On occasion she jumped around, but quickly returned to a slow gait, and a heavy-lidded disorientation. One of her eyes was a deep brown pool of softness. The other had a big blueish white spot – a piece of frozen sky, cracked by black veins. This eye was mostly blind, but she knew how to use it. And there are few things as alarming as one half-blind eye and one seeing eye looking right at you at the same time.

I brought Pearlie home to my small cabin by a creek on the outskirts of Boulder, Colorado, where I had been living and going to graduate school for two years. Pearlie had a small spot between the tulips at the front of the house that she dug out for a bed. We went for walks down the quiet little roads, slow and steady past the neighboring houses, and Pearlie rarely needed to be on a leash. She didn't often see the cats or squirrels so there wasn't much risk of her chasing them into an oncoming car, which was good because she wouldn't have noticed the car either. She walked so slowly I usually brought a book to read. Sometimes I would look up to see how she was doing, and she would be gone, having turned around and headed home on her own.

When I visited people with more normal dogs, I was always shocked. Alone, I became used to the feeling that Pearlie lived in a separate world. But in the company of other dogs, her oddness seemed extreme. She had so few typical canine qualities. She rarely wagged her tail or communicated with me in any way other than giving me that big white eye as if to plead, "This is it?" And she had a human sadness I had never seen in another animal. It was as though she was grieved by a loss I could never relieve, no matter how much I loved her.

A friend of mine once joked that Pearlie must have been a stuffed animal in a previous life because she was so soft and still. Even after coming home from the pound with those difficult years in Denver behind her, Pearlie never really had much life in her.

At home she slept most of the day. When she did get up, she would begin her routine of going out one door and coming in another. If it was winter, and the doors were closed, this meant that I had to get up and let her out. Usually she started at the side door, then she would come around the back of the house and paw at the back door. Once inside, she would take a sip of water, (even though I had a bowl outside for her) and then wait at another door for me to let her out.

I remember feeling a natural kind of hope every time I opened the door for her. As if this time she would go outside to play a bit, look for squirrels, dig up an old bone, get into some kind of dog trouble. Or, if I was letting her inside I would think, "she wants to come in and be with me, spend some time in the house." But it was never those things. She was just always on the move very, very slowly. Going nowhere. So I was always up and down, settling in and then getting up to open a door for her, finally relieved if she went into the bedroom to just sleep.

I think Pearlie knew she wasn't like other dogs. She could enter the living room and seem like a normal dog, but then she would give a look, or tilt her head, or just stare into space, and hold the pose until I was laughing at how strange she was. Then she would turn around and go back to bed.

Loving Pearlie was a challenge – she was so distant and ambiguous. I felt it was my place to seek her out, to give her love and help her receive love. It did not come easily, because even when I loved her it didn't seem to make her happy.

Since Pearlie had been abused, I never raised my voice with her. I knew I would never hurt her or scare her. Even if she frustrated me by moving too slowly or endlessly needing to go in and out of the house, I never let myself get angry. She became a living practice in kindness and care.

And very occasionally my love could make a difference. In such moments, she would roll on her back to let me pet her belly as though she enjoyed it. These times of connection meant the world to me. One of my greatest accomplishments was when I could pet Pearlie gently enough to soothe her to sleep, and walk away without her noticing I had gone. I would pet her more and more softly until her breathing was heavy and her eyelids twitched to the rhythm of her dreams. Then I would slowly pull my hand away, and tiptoe backwards until I knew she was on her own, drifting off without me, stilled into another realm by the assurances of my touch.

Although she didn't show it much, I knew Pearlie loved me. I knew somehow she was there for me, letting me love her. I wouldn't find out till much later how much she helped me, but I always knew she would stick with me no matter what.

Pearlie was not a classic beauty. But she did have a very rare quality of beauty that came with her uniqueness, and every now and then someone other than me noticed it. When that happened it was like an affirmation from the magical place Pearlie came from. A neighbor of mine in Colorado was one of the few people who saw how beautiful Pearlie was.

I was in the grocery store one day, a year or so after moving to Boulder. I had just flown back to town and I was tired. I stood at the vegetable section picking out some carrots when I noticed a woman approaching me. She wore a long skirt and her long brownish gray hair was tied back in a loose ponytail. She looked at me with gentle openness as though we were old friends.

I didn't recognize her, but I didn't feel awkward as she came closer. And I didn't even feel very surprised when she reached up and stroked my cheek. I just looked at her, confused, and asked, "Who are you?"

She said her name, and that she was my neighbor. I smiled, and said hello. There we stood, in the market by the vegetables. I was not used to being touched, but it was the most natural thing. It was as if there were no barriers between us, or between anyone, as though we could all just enter and touch each other.

A few months later in the late afternoon when the fall light was bright and cutting, Pearlie and I went out for a walk. I saw my neighbor standing at the edge of the pavement, her husband leaning against the side of their black car, which was parked half on the road and half up on the grass outside their house. His back was to his wife. She held his longish gray hair gently in her hands, and was braiding it carefully.

I walked by with Pearlie, embarrassed by such intimacy out on the street. But when I was a bit beyond them the woman tilted her head, gesturing to Pearlie and said, "She's really beautiful." I didn't know what to say, so I laughed a bit, nodded, and kept walking. Then she drew my attention back to her and said, "It's not just you who sees it."

People who saw Pearlie's beauty acted this way – as though the most intimate moment is for everyone to share, as though nothing separates us from each other, and confirmations of the most basic truths are as plenty as rain in spring.

Longing

Pearlie came into my life at a time when everything else had left.

Like many spiritual seekers, I had been given experiences in childhood that revealed the magic and power behind the veils of the ordinary. And just as mysteriously as they were given, these experiences ended, leaving a gaping hole where love had been, and a frustration at the discord between life's appearances and the mysteries hiding beneath those appearances. This haunting spiral made its first turn at summer camp when I was nine years old, and all life suddenly revealed itself as a web of unending love. A joy I had never experienced before filled my days. I don't know what those counselors were thinking, but they let the campers run around for hours unsupervised. I played card games with the girls when it rained, and I played soccer with the older boys in the afternoons. Alone, I hunted for frogs at dawn and dusk, waiting in the muddy coves to hear their songs, holding their smooth and powerful little bodies in my hands, keeping them for a little while in the small chest pockets of my green camp overalls.

I spent hours in nature, part of a magic that seemed both within and all around me. But when camp was over, and later that year unexpectedly closed down forever, that awareness of life's magic was locked behind an impenetrable barrier.

It was not easy knowing how full of love life could be, while living in love's absence. Sometimes the veils were lifted again while playing sports or hiking in the wilderness as a teenager. But those experiences could not be forced or held, and inevitably a terrible longing or boredom would take their place. After college I traveled around the country from one job or experience to the next, always searching for something unnamable. When I moved to Alaska to work at an environmental organization, the remote wildness and emptiness of that landscape awoke a driving need to come nearer and nearer to that vast power reflected all around me. I felt the best way to enter that space was to meditate. I found the opportunity at a Tibetan Buddhist monastery in Canada where I could meditate in silence for a month.

Buddhism felt familiar and welcoming to me, and its conceptual foundations were practical and profound: the human condition was generally one of suffering, but freedom from suffering was possible through practices which liberate us from attachments and align us with what is most real. The Buddha himself saw and experienced the suffering inherent in life, and eventually awakened within a state of liberation.

Reality in Buddhism is generally understood as emptiness. This emptiness is not experienced as a nihilistic negation. Rather, a dynamic and clear wisdom reveals the emptiness of all things, and a naturally arising compassion informs our actions. Thus, compassion and the wisdom of emptiness exist. The practitioner comes to know and live this wisdom and compassion through spiritual practice. And Tibetan Buddhism offered an emphasis on spiritual service that moved me deeply. Even our own liberation is renounced in our willingness to help others, as the great Buddhas and Bodhisattvas come back again and again to this earth to guide others Home.

I had confidence that Buddhist practices could help me awaken to what is real. I trusted their power. Sitting for hours in meditation helped develop a watchful, detached state of consciousness, which existed beyond my ego's thought forms and psychological dynamics. Like a gate to freedom, this detached mind was always present but never restricted by personal dramas. And the states of peace and love I experienced in meditation or while walking the wild countryside beyond the monastery grounds assured me I was on the right path. A year after that first retreat, I returned for six more months, and I met a Tibetan lama who gave me instructions in the practices of the tradition.

In those first years my commitment grew and grew. I rode a wave of excitement and self-discovery and felt compelled to do more and more practice. I discovered a Buddhist inspired school in Boulder that could train me to be a psychotherapist, and I left Alaska to enter its psychology program. I believed I had found a way to live my inner longing in a worldly profession. I wanted only to go deeper into the states of love and heightened awareness I had discovered in my own spiritual practice, and share what I learned with others.

The preliminary practices of the Tibetan Buddhist tradition were designed to engender complete commitment to the path, purify the practitioner, and help the practitioner renounce the material world and also the self.[1] This latter practice during which one symbolically offers love, harmony, riches, and oneself for the well-being of the world was especially inspiring. Not only was I offering perfection to the world, but I was offering myself in service to others. The giving of oneself is part of the journey beyond the restrictions of the world of form into the realities of non-existence.[2] This "non-existence" was what I wanted more than anything.

What was non-existence? I had no idea! I assumed it was how I felt in meditation – as though I was groundless and light, without any feelings other than devotion or peace. Reading the Buddha's words, "When you see the unborn, uncreated, unconditioned, you are liberated from everything born, created, and conditioned,"[3] I assumed he meant that freedom existed beyond this created world, like outer space exists beyond the atmosphere of the earth. I thought that non-existence was the ultimate answer to the pain of existence, and I proceeded in my practices with these deep assumptions – that spiritual practice and the love or bliss I felt in meditation would, once and for all, propel me into a place of complete freedom, far from any sadness or difficulty of life.

I had in mind that non-existence was far, far away from this ordinary world. And I looked so hard "away" that one day, at the end of one practice and the beginning of another, I realized I had followed my focus so completely that I was irretrievably lost in that "away".

I felt as though I'd left this world behind and had fallen into a horrible emptiness. This was not the vast and peaceful space I had felt in meditation, but a dissociated psycho-spiritual purgatory in which I had no access to the feelings of bliss, love, or joy that had become the basis of my experience. In fact I could feel very little other than horrified confusion. I could not fall asleep; I did not feel hunger, and I slowly weakened as though ill with an unknown disease.

I attempted the next practice – a meditation designed to help the consciousness of the disciple and guru become one, so that the teacher's mind can guide the mind of the disciple into deeper levels of reality. But I could not proceed. Something fundamental had changed. The devotion and love I felt for Tibetan Buddhism had evaporated, gone so completely it left no trace. I felt as I had so many years before when summer camp closed down. I felt confused and even betrayed. I used effort, forcing myself to practice, but it was as though I was banging my head against a wall. I could not progress, and I was lost in a black hole of meaninglessness.

Graduate school had started and I felt like a liar among true believers. I grew more and more exhausted. After a year at school still hoping that the thread of commitment would return, I let that hope finally die away.

I was devastated. I did not know what had happened or what to do with my life. Should I move? Should I try another kind of graduate program? I was too tired to even think about what was next.

One Saturday morning in spring, I sat at my white wooden kitchen table staring out the window to the creek, grown full and rough with melting winter run-off. My hands were warming around my coffee cup as the woodstove warmed the house, and I looked to the left into my neighbor's yard. She was there with her black lab, a big boy with strong legs pouncing back and forth as my neighbor tossed him a stick and clapped for his return. The light was catching the stick when it rose out of the shadows of the lilac bushes, the lab's dark coat shining in the instant that he jumped high enough to catch it. When he returned to my neighbor she held his ears in her hands and snuggled her face into the crown of that soft black head.

It took me a few minutes before I noticed I was smiling. And it took me a few days to drive to the pound and bring back Pearlie.

Pearlie and I spent a lot of time together when she came home with me. I was so lethargic I would often stay in bed till morning passed. Pearlie would jump on the bed and lie across my chest so I could rub her stomach until we were ready to get up. For many months, this was our primary way of being together. In bed or out of bed, she would come and lie across me. If I sat on the floor studying, she would look at me with her big eyes until I lay down so she could spread herself over me like a sack of potatoes pressing me to the ground. She would stay there for long periods, until her heaviness seemed part of me, assuring me I would not soon float away. Soon after bringing her home, I instinctively knew to look to Pearlie for a connection to life. I fed her, petted her, loved her. That attention and care grounded me here in this world, and somehow I understood how valuable she was to me.

I was supposed to be merging with the mind of a Buddhist lama, but instead, I merged with Pearlie.

Meeting the teacher

When I found Pearlie, my time in Colorado was coming to an end. When my spiritual life disappeared there was no reason to stay.

I felt sickened by confusion and self-doubt, unsure of what to do next. I still had many school credits, so I decided that being a psychologist was a reasonable option. I would not become a spiritual psychologist, just an ordinary psychologist working within a traditional model of the psyche. I no longer understood how spiritual energy or the love I had felt so deeply, related to my basic experiences of life. I no longer believed in spiritual life.

I spent another year with Pearlie in Boulder finishing prerequisite classes at the local university, and doing enough volunteer work to support an application to a decent program. During this time I took good care of Pearlie, bringing her on long walks and petting her belly for hours while I studied or watched television. Her softness was a balm to all the coldness that had found its place in my heart and in my life. The love between us was a slight flame that we both kept alive, like campers deep in the wilderness with only one or two matches left and no idea how long it would take to get home.

When I was accepted to a doctorate program in California, I packed the car and Pearlie and I drove away from Boulder. I sold my Colorado cabin and bought a bungalow on the east side of the San Francisco Bay. My grandfather had left me an inheritance that would pay my tuition, and allow me to not have a job. This way I could spend time with Pearlie when not at school or my internship.

The last thing on my mind was spiritual life. For two years I had lived in a kind of desert, knowing something fundamental had died and would never return. I entered my Doctorate program with only one mild interest – to do well at school and establish a decent career.

But who is to say when love will be given? Who could ever predict those currents of light and explosions of grace hovering at the edge of life just waiting for the angels to signal the invitation for love's return? Not me. But the signal must have been sent, for one day my life was changed forever.

In one of my classes at school, I met a woman I noticed and liked immediately. She was from the East Coast like me, and we felt deeply familiar to each other. Occasionally I spoke to my new friend about meditation. I told her how I had loved spiritual practice more than anything and how lost I was without it. One day, a few months after we met, we were having tea in her back yard in Berkeley. We sat under a big canvas umbrella, her small black and white cat running around the yard, Pearlie ineffectually trying to chase it, the sweetness of her garden heavy around us. And the conversation turned again to meditation.

Very slowly and carefully she said that she meditated with a Sufi group not far from where we went to school. When she mentioned this group, my body and all my inner senses became alert. I could not smell the garden; I could not taste the tea. The outer world dissolved as my inner longing erupted with a painful memory of love and belonging.

I asked her to take me to a meeting. When I walked into that ordinary house and saw my teacher sitting on a living room floor with a few people in front of him, I knew I was where I needed to be. I remember his head turned as we entered, and I looked into his eyes, which even from across the room were as vivid and precise as arrows shot by a master archer. I heard myself say, "Good. He is here," as though something could finally begin.

In that moment my connection to him was made conscious. I never doubted he was my teacher; I never questioned my com-

mitment to him. I saw in his eyes and felt in his presence an
energy that drew me like a magnet. It was as though I had been
walking in a desert for a million years and had stumbled across
a well of deep water that satiated my entire being. As though
I had been an unanswered question all my life, looking around,
anxiously attuned, crazily on edge. And here I had finally found
the answer.

From the moment I met my teacher I just wanted to be with
him. Something flowed through him – an energy or a presence
– which appealed to me more than anything I had ever experienced. It was vast and powerful and not from this world. Looking
into his blue eyes so clear and empty could transport me higher
than the highest mountain peak I had ever climbed to a place
where endless blue light and burning white snow spread out like
a frozen carpet across the earth. The freedom that was his nature,
the wild and impersonal forces that swirled around him like a
storm, disturbed and enticed me the way only something real
can do. He was so full of light. His eyes shone with galaxy after
galaxy of suns.

Being with him awoke an inner awareness that something
in my life was truly important; the emptiness I saw in his eyes
matched the utter aloneness I had felt on the glaciers of Alaska.
The freedom I experienced with him reminded me of leaving
everything behind to live at the Buddhist monastery. The joy of
finding him took me back to those bright and timeless days at
summer camp.

And there was the love. Sitting near him I could feel a warmth
flow from him and blanket us together in endless belonging, a
hundred times deeper than any warmth I had ever felt before.

Spiritual love is so hard to describe, "Love is a stranger with
a strange language,"[4] wrote Rumi of the love that ultimately annihilated his ego and dissolved him in God. Rumi was a Sufi, and

Sufism is a path of love on which the seeker is drawn by love and longing toward an unknown Beloved like a moth to a flame, until nothing of the moth or the seeker remains. I had not known love like this before I met my teacher. It was confusing and absolute, and in-arguable, like a force from a distant world. I had wanted this kind of love forever – a love that would not rise and set with my petty needs and desires, but would hold steady like an eternal sun and help awaken me within its brilliance.

A few days after meeting my teacher I understood I had the opportunity to give everything of myself for this one thing I had always wanted – spiritual life. I thought about quitting school, and I asked for guidance in that decision. I had a dream that I was at the salad bar in my school cafeteria. I had a plate in my hand, and I was looking to see what there was to eat. All the lettuce had wilted. The vegetables were old, browning at the tips.

Dream-work is part of the Sufi tradition, a modern version of Sufism's ancient teaching stories, and we always followed meditation with tea and dream-work. I told my dream in the group, and my teacher confirmed what I had thought – that the school could offer me nothing and something else of great value was being offered – and with his encouragement I moved near the retreat center of his Sufi lineage.

In the West we have few examples of spiritual discipleship. We can read the Bible, and hear Jesus' words to his Apostles encouraging them to leave their lives behind and "Come with Me.[5]" But it seems our world has forgotten this degree of commitment and devotion. When I met my teacher, something inside me remembered.

I found a tenant for my East Bay house and Pearlie and I moved into a vacation house tucked into the same mountain ridge that held the meditation center a mile down the road. It was damp and drafty, and was filled with the owner's strange looking collectables from Africa. But I didn't care. I was so happy to be there. Nothing mattered to me but this new closeness to my teacher and the love I felt between us. And it was not long before the landlords who owned my teacher's house offered me a house for very low rent, and I moved in, feeling deeply cared for. That little house overlooking a field of cows was perfect for Pearlie and me, and for the wild kitten I found in the bushes one day.

Soon I was spending so much time with my teacher. We meditated alone together, or took long walks on the ridge behind the center, talking like old friends. The first four or five months I was there, the retreat center was closed to visitors and it felt as though I was his only student. But even when guests began to arrive he always kept time for me, joining me alone in an empty room where we would sit and talk or meditate. It seemed natural to spend so much time together. When he told me my life was about helping him in his work, and he asked me to edit his books, I knew I was in the right place. My path was marked by such inner intimacy and outer nearness with my teacher that at times I felt like the luckiest person in the world.

But the path was not only about this love and belonging. And in those years near my teacher he began to show me love's hidden partner – a disturbing inner emptiness where personal fulfillment is impossible.

Some days I would be overtaken by an awareness of complete inner desolation and nothingness. I would go to the center and sit and cry or try to meditate. Sometimes I was there alone. Other times, my teacher would join me. Often he made my feelings of desolation disappear with his stories and his love, but sometimes he made them worse. One morning he came to the center and sat next to me, bowed his head, and let his clear blue eyes water with sadness. "My teacher always had tears in his eyes," he said before he walked away and left me alone.

These intense and contrasting experiences – comfort and coldness, fear and love, belonging and aloneness – existed in one place, in my relationship to my teacher. And underneath all those paradoxes was an even more essential state of surrender I had been made aware of years before.

Eight years earlier I had been meditating in my fisherman's shack on the Alaskan coast when I was somehow taken out of my body to a different dimension. This had never happened before, or since. I watched as my consciousness slowly spliced into another time and place, like a choppy transition from one frame of a movie to another.

Suddenly I stood on a landing on the second floor of a house. Terrified and confused, I walked with great trepidation down the hall when I suddenly felt a frightening power behind me. A man was quietly standing there. His presence evoked the greatest fear I had known. I stood, gripping a stairway railing, unable to turn around. Eventually, with no other option, I mustered my courage and turned to face him.

In an instant, I no longer existed. But I was on the ground at his feet. I had no human body; but I could see. All I saw were the black lace-up shoes of the man I had tried to face. I was nothing. I was less than the dust on the floor at his feet. Staring at those shoes, in shock and confusion, I became aware for the first time in my life that I was absolutely powerless before a someone I had yet to meet in the ordinary world.

Propelled by fear, I desperately drew my mind back into my ordinary self, and I returned to normal consciousness, sitting in my cabin, scared and disoriented.

As with other mystical experiences, I did not understand what had happened to me. But it left a lasting impression. I had met a powerful force. I believed somewhere there was a great spiritual being who knew me, and I longed to know him. Always, though,

I had been confused by this odd experience of seeming to have no body, being only part of the floor at his feet.

Years later I came to know that realizing one is less than dust at the feet of the teacher is a classic experience on the spiritual path. A Saint in our lineage once sat in the garden of her teacher, a great Indian Guru, as he quietly recited the words to an ancient poem:

> *A sweet smell has the dust at the feet of my Guru; never I cried before, but now there is no end of sorrow for me.*[6]

With my teacher I began to live from this space of inner surrender, a space of sweetness and also sorrow where one is absolutely bowed down before something vast and powerful. And later, when my teacher pushed me away from him, he offered a way to live this uncompromising devotion no matter where I was or who I was with.

The Sufis

I had loved Buddhism so much, that I was surprised to discover that my teacher was a Sufi. If I were to have envisioned my teacher, I would have conjured up an old Buddhist monk – a wise, bearded ascetic, living alone in a monastic retreat hut or somewhere in the woods. But here he was only ten years older than me, married to a beautiful woman, father of two, driving a Honda around a little town north of San Francisco.

It was all so unsettling – meeting the Sufis.

I had taken a couple of college courses about Sufism, and other than feeling the beauty of a spiritual tradition founded on the power of love, I was not very interested. I felt drawn to the simplicity and ascetic qualities of Buddhism. Sufis are passionate lovers of God; Sufi literature is filled with poetry and songs of love for the Beloved, another word for God. Words like *"the Beloved"* and *"God"* had never rung true to me. It was the Buddhist stories of living in caves, meditating all day in the vast and clear emptiness, and eating only nettles that inspired my devotion. Those people meant business! The Sufis spoke of softening the heart so that it became as warm as wool. But I had tended toward the hard and disciplined model of spiritual life.

Of course all this changed as soon as I was loved beyond my imaginings. How quickly I lost the hard dignity of asceticism! How quickly I came to feel that *"God"* was the only word to describe the intimate and all-powerful energy that knew me so well and claimed me so completely. All it took was love.

But in the beginning, I found it confusing to be in a group of Sufis.

Our group included approximately thirty people from the Bay Area, and many from other states and even Europe. The retreat center, which consisted of three ordinary houses strung midway up a hillside ridge of Bay trees, could accommodate ten or fifteen visitors at a time, and it was almost always filled.

But it was not really a "community" of people. Visitors could only stay for a few weeks. A few people lived near the center, either invited to work for my teacher, as only three or four people had been, or encouraged to move there, as I had been, under vaguer premises. A few others simply lived nearby and went on with their own lives, unrelated to his work. But there were no "followers" or "groupies" for people did not give up their lives to be near the teacher. I seemed to have been the exception to that rule.

Our group met two times a week for meditation, tea and cookies, and then dream-work. I loved the silent meditation, but I was surprised to see that many of the people lay down to meditate, sat on soft couches, or slumped over onto cushions and blankets. I was used to meditating with a straight back for hours at a time, with no movement at all. Eventually I understood that we weren't really meditating, but rather we were doing a form of yogic relaxation that helps one's consciousness be absorbed into a greater consciousness, so it can be used. It did not really matter how one sat, for the body was left behind. I came to love meditating with this group, and how I could find myself drifting into a deep and endless silence.

At first I did not like the dream-work. I had been a vivid dreamer at times, and had occasionally kept dream journals, but I had never really learned to pay attention to my dreams, and didn't quite trust them, feeling they were just another form of fantasy. I much preferred the silence of meditation, the purity of that inner engagement and absorption.

Slowly I began to appreciate dream-work. In time, the group showed me how to discriminate between levels of dreams. I saw how some psychological dreams come from the mind and ego-conditioning, and some from a vaster cultural conditioning – what Carl Jung called "the collective unconscious." Other dreams emanate from the magical archetypal realms, and others belong to the plane of the Higher Self, or soul. There are also teaching dreams, in which one's soul is given an experience by the teacher or another master on the path. During dream-work we trained our minds to be attentive to qualities and energies beyond the ego, and let those energies and experiences guide us in our lives.

It was not just the meditation and dream work that confused me in those first months and even years with the Sufis. I did not understand why everyone had husbands and wives and children. I didn't know how someone could love another human being, when this love between the disciple and teacher was so great. And how could one meditate most of the day if they had to go to work and take care of children?

I had taken monastic vows at the Buddhist monastery, and even though they were temporary they seemed to fit me well. Tibetan Buddhism is traditionally a monastic path, emphasizing months and even years in retreat to allow one's consciousness to detach from this world and slowly awaken beyond the illusions of ordinary perception. But my teacher's lineage of Sufism does not emphasize monasticism. In fact, my new friends on the path almost all had families and ordinary jobs. This made no sense to my ascetic nature, and to my focus on spiritual practice. The Sufis had only to meditate for a half hour or so every day, and try to remember God in their hearts. These were the main practices of our lineage, and it was hard for me to believe it was enough. But I often heard our teacher emphasize grace rather than effort. "Spiritual things are given," he would say. Effort and intention had their place, but grace was the real power on the path.

One thing both Buddhism and Sufism share is the importance of the teacher. I had once attempted a Buddhist practice designed to help me merge with the consciousness of my Tibetan lama, to facilitate the journey into deeper levels of reality. Sufism also emphasizes merging with the teacher. The Sufi Saint Bhai Sahib once said, *"If you are being merged into the Teacher, you will know God."*[7]

But unlike in Tibetan Buddhism, this mystery does not happen through any particular practice. Whereas I had attempted specific visualizations and mantra recitations during my Buddhist practices, with the Sufis I had nothing particular to do. On our path, so much happens deep on the level of the soul, far from the awareness of the ordinary mind. The esoteric mystery of merging happens over time, through the power and grace of the tradition. The disciple lives her ordinary life, continuing with the few practices of meditation and remembrance, and being in the presence of the teacher from time to time.

It was this emphasis on ordinary life that disturbed me the most. A basic principle of the lineage my teacher represents is *"Outwardly to be with the people, inwardly to be with God.*[8]*"* This is the training I saw others surrender to: to be hidden in plain sight, to love God in the midst of the marketplace. The comforts of isolation and long retreat were not allowed on our path. These seekers mixed their desire for God and love for the truth into the world of commerce and politics, families and worldly joys and responsibilities.

But I was glad not to have to take that step. I was grateful to be able to stay by my teacher's side with few outer responsibilities. This one relationship of devotion made sense to me like nothing else had, and I lived it fully as though it would never end.

The back door

From the moment I met my teacher, Pearlie and my love for her became lost in the shadows of my devotion to him. Her slowness and simplicity held no sway in light of so much love and power. Walks with her took me away from the meditation center. Her need for me meant I could not go on overnight retreats. I resented her somewhat, but mostly I just forgot her. And one day I had the idea to give her away so she could live with someone who could love her more than I could.

It was so natural and so easy to want to give her away. She wasn't even a happy dog. She barely wagged her tail for me, and didn't even seem to need me much. I thought she would be a good match for an older person who could be with her all day long – two old deaf companions, resting, watching television; just being together.

So a few months after moving near my teacher, I placed an ad in the paper of the nearest city and put notices on the bulletin boards in the little town where I lived.

No one called.

About a week after I placed the ad, I was petting Pearlie in the back of my car in the meditation center's parking lot, waiting for the cars blocking us to leave. My teacher was walking down the driveway, but when he saw us he stopped and approached. He leaned against the blue car in the afternoon light and just watched. After a moment, he said that this love I had with Pearlie, this simple and human love, was very important. I told him I wanted to give her away, but he shook his head, and insisted that I didn't. "You need this kind of love," he said, smiling gently.

What for? I wondered. What did this simple love for a dog have to do with anything? What did it have to do with spiritual life? I had no idea. But I did what he said and I kept Pearlie. And a few days later my teacher called me over after meditation and said to me, "Don't forget, God enters through the back door."

He was reminding me that God enters our lives where we least expect it, where we are not looking, through the forgotten and rejected places. At that moment, I did not really understand why he was telling me this. But later I had to admit that in my case, God entered in the back door, went out the front, came back in the side door, and around again and again...

As above, so below

There is an old Sufi teaching that God said, "I am with those whose hearts are broken for my sake."[9] When I met my teacher my heart had never been broken. But two years after moving near him, that process began. The hours alone with him became fewer and fewer. He had assured me that my life was about working with him, but he gave me less and less to do. Others moved to our small town and were given jobs in his office, while I was left alone. His caring assurances were replaced by impatience as I looked to him for help with my life. His love turned to coldness, until my loneliness nearly swallowed me completely.

His coldness worked on my heart and psyche, eroding thought structures and emotional need in the acid of his absence. The more he ignored me, the more inner pain, despair and anger arose. These were years of work on myself as my consciousness tried to contain and transform that darkness.

I was not doing this work alone. This ancient tradition I was now a part of was helping more than I knew. Walking from the parking area to the meditation center one day with my teacher and a visitor, I was shown this grace. Along the road, my teacher ignored me while being so kind to the guest, and I filled with sadness. When the guest walked on and left my teacher and me alone together, I asked him, "Why do I have to feel so much pain around you?" His expression changed from coldness to warmth suddenly, as though he had just been allowed to tell me something. He said, softly, his clear blue eyes filled with compassion, "So I can breathe love on it."

Then I understood that when my pain rose to the surface it was held in a container of love and attention that ultimately helped transform it. And it was not just my own consciousness doing this work. The light and power of our tradition was the greater force transforming my own inner darkness, as it was with others on the path.

This inner work was so painful, but I had been warned. I had been warned that I would have to lose something of my love for my teacher if I was to awaken to deeper spiritual truths. In my first year near him, I dreamed about the alchemical mystery of oneness:

> *I am walking with my teacher down the road near our meditation center. I am filled with love for him.*
>
> *At one point he stops, and I stand next to him. He points up ahead, showing me a small waterfall. Water cascades down dark rocks and flows into a stream at the edge of the road. At the same time we can hear through a culvert or a drainage grate water flowing underground. I hear a voice ask, "Does the water above flow from the same source as the water below?"*
>
> *But I am so dizzy with love for my teacher that I cannot discern the question. I cannot answer. In fact, I do not care about the question. I am just so happy to be with him.*

In the ancient text *The Emerald Tablet* Hermes wrote of the journey of consciousness:

> *It rises from earth to heaven, so as to draw the lights of the heights to itself, and descends to the earth; thus within it are the forces of the above and the below"*[10]

My dream warned that something of my love for my teacher was getting in the way of my stepping into the reality of oneness, the realization that life here on earth is fed by the same divine source as life beyond this world. My attention, my aspirations, seemed caught in a higher love, and had not taken the journey of descent, as indicated by Hermes, which ultimately would bring together the forces of the higher and the lower.

When I awoke from my dream, I did not think I cared as much about oneness as I did for my teacher. When I was with my teacher I was not even slightly interested in that great alchemical mystery of life: *"Does the water above flow from the same source as the water below?"* All I wanted was the love between us.

Could I really believe I would have to let go of that love? And could I imagine that my utterly compelling love for him who was so empty and beautiful was essentially the same as my love for my dog who was so plodding and simple?

No, I could not believe it.

But I was on a path that took one deeper and deeper into the heart, and my teacher was not the ultimate destination for the devotion that lived inside me. The love was needed somewhere else. Where was this hidden need? Somewhere in the mystery beyond my own attachments, beyond the appearances of my teacher's presence and absence, a place Pearlie – not my teacher – could show me.

It was such a long time before I allowed Pearlie to reveal what was deep and true in both of us. I had to leave so much behind along the way, and was often unsure and unhappy about what I was being given.

Where did this journey start? It is hard to find just the moment, because it seemed to be without beginning or end. But there was a point, almost five years after moving to California, when Pearlie was dying. We can start there.

2

Sand in the oyster

O Hafiz, if you are seeking
the pearl of union, do this:
From tears, make yourself
an ocean and then dive![11]

Hafiz

The beginning

It was swimming weather – hot and bright – the September day Mary, our vet, called to tell me Pearlie had cancer. The previous week I had taken Pearlie in because I felt a lump near her stomach. Mary operated the same day and removed a tumor and Pearlie's lymph nodes, in case the tumor was malignant and cancer had spread.

Pearlie and I had been out with my friend Nan and her dog Pilgrim swimming in the bay for a few hours that afternoon. The small town in California where I lived was surrounded by water. There was an ocean on one side of the ridge and a bay on the other. Nan meditated with our group and lived nearby with her husband Roger, another good friend, and every Wednesday Nan and I went to the other side of the bay and walked on our favorite spit of land with our dogs. This day was hot enough to swim so we left our clothes on a sandy slope and joined the seals and cormorants out in the salty waters.

Nan's dog Pilgrim, a flat coated retriever, was a great swimmer and he looked noble and horse-like, charging through the water. Pearlie didn't swim, but she would go right into the water so that the little waves just touched her belly. She would stand there while the water gently swooshed her fur to one side and then back to the other, looking with contentment to the horizon, for as long as we wanted to swim.

That afternoon Pearlie and I returned to a message on my machine from Mary asking me to call her. When I heard the tone of her voice I knew something was wrong. She told me that the lump from Pearlie's stomach was cancer. The tests on Pearlie's lymph node revealed that the cancer had already spread. She said we could do chemotherapy, but even with treatment, which itself was so taxing for nine-year old dog, the cancer would most likely return. She knew from years of caring for Pearlie that Pearlie was a sensitive dog, disturbed by being with anyone other than me and unwilling to endure much discomfort at another's hands. We both agreed the chemotherapy did not make sense. She said Pearlie had three to six months to live.

I hung up the phone and sat on my yellow couch, staring out across the fields. Black and white cows were feeding and bright egrets shone through the green marsh grasses. The shock brought out a vividness to everything, as though I could see every blade of grass, every feather on every water bird. I stared on and on before the despair set in.

At first I was too sad to tell anyone about Pearlie's cancer. I was afraid to speak of it, fearing I would just collapse like someone whose bones had been suddenly sucked away by an invisible monster. It wasn't really that I was sorry to see Pearlie go. Rather, it was just that another loss seemed unbearable in the loneliness following my teacher's withdrawal.

For a week or two I stayed alone with my despair. But then I told some friends, and one friend told my teacher. Soon after, in front of our meditation group, he suggested that I write a book about her.

I was dizzy with incomprehension. I had been his editor and I had even written a book, but I had never thought of myself as a writer, and had no interest in writing. More importantly, I had little interest in Pearlie. My love for my teacher had long overshadowed my love for her. I did not begin to write about her, and a week later, my teacher mentioned it again. He told me to attend to Pearlie, and Pearlie would take me to God.

One might think that this would feel encouraging to me, or inspiring. I was, after all, on a spiritual path. This was what I said I had always wanted – to know what was real within life and within myself. And I tried to remind myself of this. But my teacher's instructions didn't inspire me; they ushered in a sense of total devastation. Writing a book about Pearlie meant months or years alone in my house, first with a dying dog then with nothing and no one. Perhaps God existed in that complete aloneness, but even the thought of stepping through the outer netherworlds of loneliness to reach that inner prize was terrifying.

Our teacher had often told our group that no one is given more than he or she can bear, and no one is told to do something that he or she cannot do. But I was not sure how to begin. And there was nothing appealing about beginning.

I tried to believe that Pearlie could take me to realization. I went back and forth from the gentle and cool surrender of faith to the burning of my inner need, hoping that one day the terrible tension between these poles would be resolved. I was often ashamed that I did not care more about Pearlie and the hidden mysteries I could only imagine she embodied. But I could not do it. I could not choose the emptiness and aloneness she represented over my devotion to my teacher.

At the end of a meditation meeting, a few weeks after my teacher suggested I attend to Pearlie, I was beginning to put away my cushion and blanket when my teacher turned to me very quickly and said, "Hilary, do you remember those final words from the Buddha to his disciples?" I looked at him a bit dazed, surprised to hear him speak to me. He lifted his head upwards, smiling so fully as though enraptured, and said, "Buddha's last words were: *Be a light unto yourself, betake yourself to no external refuge. Hold fast to the Truth!*"

Then he got up and walked out of the room.

This was the time, he was telling me, to claim my own inner light and my own connection to God and live it fully.

I had needed my teacher's presence to know the love that flowed in my own heart. I had needed his absence to burn away my pettiness and reflect the silent emptiness of my own being. But my time discovering my self through my relationship to him was over. Far beyond my awareness I had said "yes" to this path that would take me into my own light whether I liked it or not. And discovering my own light seemed to have something to do with discovering Pearlie's light. So I began to do what my teacher suggested and look to her.

Surrendering to life

I could not imagine what kind of light burned inside Pearlie that could match the light of my teacher. He had split me open with love and need – bringing me to states of union and belonging, vulnerability and despair, beyond anything I had known. He had brought meaning and value to my life. But with Pearlie, that meaning disappeared as though it had never been given. My spiritual life was sacrificed in an unfair bargain and all that remained was a dying dog. Where was the light in that?

I had always assumed spiritual life was a way out of the banality of ordinary life. I was part of a spiritual lineage of Sufis annihilated in love, and I had heard the stories of seekers being absorbed in God – the moth destroyed by the flame. This crazy suffering of the ego in the flames of love appealed to me, and when I experienced the burning of unmet need with my teacher it felt familiar and acceptable despite its inherent pain. I liked the wildness of the path, the sense that something truly exciting was taking place. As I endured the pain, I knew it was for a greater purpose. But suddenly I was without purpose. Suddenly there was nothing to endure. My teacher's attention, which had contained my suffering and infused it with meaning, was gone.

Alone with Pearlie I slowly realized that I had misunderstood something about the ego's annihilation. I had imagined it as a wild process resulting in a finale of spiritual success. I imagined ongoing and deepening bliss and ecstasy. I thought of it as an end to the obligations of ordinary life, just as I had assumed, so many years earlier when I first began practicing Buddhism, that non-existence meant freedom from existence. But now I realized that the death of the ego had something to do with Pearlie – something to do with her ordinariness and gentle softness, with how much a part of life she was. And it was hard for me to acknowledge just how much I feared all these things.

Everyone has a closet in her house with a box tied up in the back, hiding that which she most dislikes or fears, and wants most to ignore. For me, the box contained everything "ordinary." I had never liked ordinary life, and was always drawn toward thrilling challenges that tested and pushed me. But now my teacher had forced me to stare ordinariness right in the face and give myself to it completely. And all that face did was stare back at me blankly, that one eye demanding in its nearly blind ambiguity.

What was I to do with Pearlie? She didn't seem to want anything new, or need to do anything herself. She just slept all day. If she was inside she had a mild interest in lunch or snacks. Outside she mostly rested under the wild rose bush in her spot of cool, dug-out earth. One day I went outside to find her, hoping to see the divine message I assumed was trying to be delivered. The neighbor had left her sprinkler on for too long, and Pearlie's dug-out hole had filled with water. But there was Pearlie, looking at me with a simple "hello" as though everything was as it should be, even as her paws and chest were submerged in mud. I just shook my head and laughed.

After I rinsed the mud off Pearlie's belly and legs with my own hose, she lay on the living room floor and I lifted her scraggly chin in my hands. I focused on her one good eye to get her attention, and looked again for answers. But Pearlie was Pearlie; she had never been concerned with inquiry. She wrested her head from my hands and put it back on the floor.

The dullness and endlessness of those early days with Pearlie were nearly suffocating, and I almost could not bear it. Up the road my teacher undertook his important spiritual work with those he asked to help him, while I was left alone with a bored and dying dog.

The only time she seemed to want anything was when I sat down to meditate and just as I closed my eyes she would come over and nudge my arm with her spongy nose. The slightest pressure from that gentle and demanding nose and meditation was over.

I wasn't sure what to do with Pearlie, so we just sat together or went for walks. At first there was so much disappointment and loneliness between us that it took great effort to be with her. But I tried. I tried to look at her with fresh eyes, hoping to find a hidden meaning in her simplicity and slowness. I even started a program of new activities. At least two or three days a week we walked on new beaches and trails. I did not allow myself to bring books to read, but instead I watched Pearlie carefully.

And every now and then she showed me something – like the morning we walked down a hillside a few miles from our house and were suddenly overtaken by two fast hiking men. We were descending a steep and narrow trail, and Pearlie was in front of me. I let the men with their fancy hiking clothes pass me, but then there was Pearlie.

The trail was so steep that Pearlie's bottom stuck right up in the air, waddling slowly from one side of the trail to the next as she gingerly and methodically stepped on the rough rocks. She would stop and sniff the bushes here and there, oblivious to anything but these new smells. The men were stuck. I smiled to myself the whole way down the hill as they tried to pass Pearlie. But the trail was just too narrow, and Pearlie was not a slim dog.

One man turned to me for an explanation, and I said, "Oh, she's an old dog, and a bit blind and deaf. There isn't anything I can do to move her along." He stared bewildered and annoyed, and we all took our time slowly descending the hill, Pearlie an unlikely leader, completely unaware of the activities in the rear.

Sitting alone at dinner that night I looked at Pearlie sleeping in her bed near the couch, not even concerned with table scraps. Just sleeping. A little snore every now and then, and some twitching paws. And in the subtle emptiness of that moment, I realized Pearlie symbolized everything I had avoided since meeting my teacher.

My project to be with Pearlie was masterfully designed, for she was everything I did not want. She was the opposite of what I expected and hoped for. She was slow and dull, heavy and smelly.

But I loved her.

This was the strangest truth – that momentary universal laughter. For while I did not love Pearlie as much as I loved my teacher, and the love seemed so different, I did love her.

And I knew something about love. I knew that in love there is surrender. Surrender to what? I wondered that evening. I did not know. But even that question was lost in gentle laughter.

Everything was lost in that laughter.

Wholeness

That night lying in bed I began to understand why my teacher told me to relate to Pearlie. It was because she was already complete. I certainly didn't have any plans for her, any ambitions or hopes. She was the one thing that I did not include in my spiritual aspirations. I let her be.

She *just was*.

How could I experience what the Buddhists call "pure being" if I rejected the part of my self and my life that *is*? How could I experience the presence of God if I could not experience the part of myself that is *present*?

Pearlie was present and complete, there was nothing to add to her or take away from her. Perhaps that's why I wanted to give her away when I came to my teacher. I hadn't yet learned the value of something that has no value other than being itself. I still thought value required achievement or skillful execution. I thought real value was found at the end of striving and transforming. But Pearlie reflected a wholeness much more powerful and mysterious than that which can be achieved through doing or striving.

I had a friend in the Sufi group named Barbara. She had a dog, a sweet black dog named Bear, and the four of us sometimes went for walks together. When Barbara heard I was writing a book about Pearlie, she lent me a small book about Sufism and dogs. In Sufi symbolism, dogs can represent the energies of the lower or instinctual nature. On the Sufi path, as on many spiritual paths, these natures must be purified. But this book hints at a way to purify the lower that does not reject it, but gives it a place in the wholeness of the human being. The great first century Sufi Saint Bayazid Bistami tells a story of how the lower and higher come together in spiritual transformation. One day Bayazid meets a dog on the road and says:

"You are outwardly impure and I inwardly. Come let us put the two together so that the combination will bring purity to both of us." The dog then said, "You are not worthy of my companionship, for I am rejected by mankind while you are accepted. Stones are thrown at me while you are greeted as the "Monarch of the Gnostics.' I never leave so much as a bone for tomorrow but you have a whole crock of wheat stored up." Bayazid replied, "If I am not a worthy companion to a dog, how can I accompany the Eternal? Glory be to God Who cultivates the finest of creation through the basest thereof!"[12]

I loved this little parable, and I could somehow hear Pearlie, like the dog speaking to Bayazid, telling me something about my own nature and how to relate to it. I had been rejecting my own ordinary nature, my dense and simple needs. I had thrown stones at the parts of myself I did not like and thought were not "spiritual" enough. Hadn't I even tried to give Pearlie away? But as the story says, this lower part has its place in the realization of God. For "one cannot accompany the Eternal" if one cannot accompany a dog.

What does this mean, I wondered – a God who "cultivates the finest of creation through the basest thereof?" What does it mean to bring the lower together with the higher? The un-spiritual with the spiritual? I wasn't sure, but if anyone could show me how to be a worthy companion to a dog, it was Pearlie.

New love

Over the winter months I began to feel something changing. Something new was coming. For a long time this newness remained vague, like Pearlie. It was easy to miss, like a dandelion in a field of orange poppies.

A different way of seeing – or a different sense altogether – was needed to see what Pearlie was trying to show me. As new as it was to me, it seemed an ancient love. Eyes might miss a splash of yellow in field of orange poppies, but love would not. Love would know that dandelion because everything is unique in love; all parts of life are loved for what they are.

I had given myself to love. It had been around for so many years in so many forms – its wildness consuming me, its violence finding hidden places nothing else could reach. But now I was gambling on another side of love; I was placing my bet on love's simpler, silent twin. After all, Pearlie was simple. Wouldn't I need a simple love to really know her?

One morning warm already with the wood stove and the rising winter sun, I sat on my couch and closed my eyes, letting myself drift beyond the parts of myself that were jumpy with pain and need. I sank down through the complexities of my despair until I could feel no more discomfort and hear no more complaints. There in the darkness I felt around for Pearlie. I followed my love here and there, through breezes and whisperings, into echoes and warm rain.

There she was glowing gently in the silence. Alive and still. Love wrapped us both in a blanket of belonging like a small wave lifts up the sand and swirls it back into itself.

This love for Pearlie was part of a gentle wholeness, softened with peace.

I had to be still and very patient to feel it. I could not force myself there. I had to ask for this love and open towards it. And if it revealed itself, its sweet currents seemed to stream through the air and I could ride them deeper into love like a pair of birds rides a sunset home to nest.

Just like Pearlie, this new love had its own ways and would not be bullied. It was slow and heavy, like the deepest part of a wide river. To feel it, I had to stop thinking. There were no questions there, and no puzzles to solve. Just like Pearlie, there was no mind. After all, she was not a smart girl.

This love was so much like Pearlie. It was both of a far away place and also just here, with nothing particular to offer. When Pearlie looked at me with nothing to say, the love was there. When she came over to me and just stood, not even wanting to be petted, but I used my fingers anyway to find, through her wiry outer fur, that downy undercoat, it was there. When we went for walks and the sun was just gone and the evening was new with tender shadows and Pearlie meandered onward like a Pearl rolling slowly from an open palm, the love was there.

Sometimes the love was bright and soft as late-summer light, when the sun is so subtle and the reeds and tall grasses are already turning hay-brown or golden yellow. You can catch glimpses when you don't look straight ahead of strings of reflecting light – those flying baby spider filaments crossing the sky on a breeze, shining on slow wind, waiting to land somewhere and be spun into new life.

This is how it was in the beginning. I tried to sit quietly and wait. I had to be careful, and listen. I had to be still enough to catch sight of those little streams of light, so fine they were easy to miss. Those little threads would be the story Pearlie would tell me – a story of light and life, a story of being and of weaving.

So, I attended to Pearlie. I looked in myself for love, and then I looked to her and let the love flow. I wrapped her in love and kept her warm with love. When I told myself Pearlie was the most important thing, I tried to made sure my doubts could not express their complaints. I held a space so that when Pearlie decided to tell me her secrets, I would be able to hear her.

As I practiced seeing Pearlie there was more and more to see. One day it was a new quality to her coat – a new shine. Another day it was a new tenderness. Whatever it was it was so simple. It was very, very quiet. When it made noise, it was like a soft humming, or the voice of an old woman on a porch singing songs of hidden hills and springs and ancestors. A gentle, gentle, back and forth – not the song or the chair against the wood, just the back and forth over and over again.

This new quality showed up in a quiet place between us when we were really together. When it was just me and my soft white dog with the black lines around her eyes and her giant, cool moist nose.

And I took care to notice how Pearlie's presence affected other people, like when my friend Seana came over for dinner. Seana and I were dear friends, but she did not really like dogs, and, like everyone else, she was put off by Pearlie's bad breath. But Pearlie liked Seana, and had the habit of coming right up to Seana when she visited. I had a small low table, and we sat on pillows on the floor to eat. This meant that when Pearlie approached she was right there at eye level.

This night, Seana and I were talking and laughing over our salmon and mashed potatoes. Pearlie came out of the bedroom and came up to Seana and stared at her a few inches from her face. Seana was so polite and she knew how much I loved Pearlie. She did not want to offend me. But I could tell that she did not like having Pearlie so close with that breath and her demanding presence. She recoiled a bit and tried to turn her head away to discourage Pearlie. But Pearlie just stood there staring at Seana.

Watching this standoff. I was embarrassed suddenly, feeling how unpleasant Pearlie's presence was for Seana. I was embarrassed to have a dog with such bad breath. But Pearlie would not move! The moment seemed to last forever. Everyone was uncomfortable. Except for Pearlie who stood there with unearthly persistence as though delivering an important message no one was willing to receive.

But then, suddenly, Seana's whole face opened up like a sudden sunrise. She smiled at Pearlie. I guess there was just nothing else to do. We both laughed and laughed and Seana petted Pearlie.

Then, Pearlie turned around and went back to bed as though her work was done.

I watched Pearlie carefully for more clues, signs, and ways to enter what I began to call our laughing secret. Because even though the love between Pearlie and me was simple and still, it had a laughter to it, as though Pearlie herself had a sense of humor.

Later that week we went for a walk around the neighborhood and I brought a book to read, as she had been particularly slow-moving that day. At the bend beyond my house, where the blackberry bushes become their fullest I looked up from my book, and Pearlie was not there. I was scared that she might be lost or hurt. So I turned around and ran back. But there she was, just ambling up the street heading home.

I caught up to her, ran in front of her, and looked her straight in the eyes as if to say, "What are you doing, Pearlie? Are you really that old and tired?"

Suddenly she got down on her front paws, shook her head to the side, looked at me with some new wildness, and ran past me, going this way and that, careening from one side of the road to the other! When I ran after her, she just went faster and faster, here and there, until she was going around in circles. Then, breaking away she ran all the way home and I followed her stumbling with my own laughing.

Spiders and hags

My love for Pearlie grew, but inevitably my loneliness would take its turn. One day I was lost in peace and simplicity, the next I was lost in sorrow. One day life seemed a gentle garden, and the next I felt caught in an alley of emptiness, the ghosts of my past swarming around me, grabbing at my pockets like hungry orphans on a street corner.

Sometimes I let myself live with the hope that my teacher still had a place for me near him. Even a dysfunctional relationship was a relationship. Even ghosts kept hallways busy and full. But being with ghosts made me anxious and bored. And into that boredom entered two powerful figures from my inner world: the Spider and the Hag, waking me up with disgust and then curiosity, tempting me to understand something deeper about myself and my resistance to life.

During my years in California I had many spider dreams, and that winter I dreamt of a giant black and hairy spider running around my kitchen. I was panicked and tried again and again to smash it with a pan but it was too fast. I awoke in a state of anxiety and disgust.

That panic was part of my state of being for many weeks. A deep terror and anxiety often kept me from really connecting to Pearlie. I was so afraid of something – but what? I felt sorry for my distance from her, even though she did not seem to notice. I prayed for clues about this anxiety and for ways to resolve it. One night I awoke to hear a voice telling me: "It's all about Sleeping Beauty."

Sleeping Beauty is the tale of the Princess who is put to sleep when pricked by a poisoned spindle. Why is she poisoned? The King does not invite a fairy hag to his daughter's christening, and the hag enacts revenge with a deadly curse. Another fairy lessens the curse, and Sleeping Beauty does not die from the poison, but sleeps for a hundred years.

I understood the tale to be about the maturation of feminine power and the place of the dark hag-like feminine energy in that process. The Princess is the key character, the girl who can individuate into a spiritually mature woman. But her development is stunted by the fairy hag, who is enraged at not being invited to the christening.

When a dark power is not included in spiritual life, it works against spiritual growth. This was what I was being told in the night.

The King was not the only one trying to keep a girl's spiritual development pure and sweet. I shared his patriarchal prejudices for spiritual purity, the light of consciousness, and transcendent spiritual ideals. A part of me still wanted to be where my teacher was – totally detached from this world and absorbed in the emptiness of non-being, about which I had so often read. I did not want to be involved with anything hag-like. Ugliness, woodsy-ness, darkness, crudeness, warts and crooked teeth – all these qualities I associated with the Hag. She represented a dimension of life that was fully earthbound, and even underground, and it was hard to see what this dimension had to do with spiritual evolution, which I had always imagined as a process of transcending the earth and all the limitations of this world.

But I had learned from years on a spiritual path watching how people change and grow, or not grow, that energies within the personal or collective consciousness that are not valued or given their rightful place will retreat into the unconscious, stay hidden in the shadows. In the darkness of the unconscious they can become forces at work against life and growth, just as the fairy hag, rejected and disdained, inhibited the Princess' growth.

The Hag was like those spiders who were entering my dreams with their hairy legs and thick bodies. Like the fairy hag, the weapon of the spider is poison, paralyzing her prey – even her mate and young – ensuring her own isolation and power. Life for the prey is frozen in time, out of the unpredictable flow of real life. These inner forces were keeping me in a web so that I could not move, just as the Princess was paralyzed in sleep.

I could feel this frozen-ness then, in how I was caught between my attachment to my teacher and an unknown world. I was unable to step into a life without his support and the old love between us. And I could feel it in how I was unable to really give myself to Pearlie. I felt stuck and frustrated, trapped by my own unwillingness to let go.

I heard the spiders and hags when I tried to love Pearlie and surrender into her simplicity. There could be moments of peace and acceptance, but then mean, old witch-like voices made nasty declarations that nothing good would ever come to me, and all would be best if Pearlie just died, right then and there. When I heard these voices, I longed to turn back to how things had been instead of forward into the unknown. Back toward the vast shining light of my teacher, a light beyond the dense earth. I did not want to lose that light, or step away from the monastery of my own making into an outer world where I was less protected and so alone.

I had a task before me, a task that was part of surrendering to life and stepping closer to Pearlie. The task was to face these dark archetypal forces of the Spider and Hag and uncover their mysterious power. I could not keep rejecting them, for rejected they stayed in their position of power deep in my psyche. There had to be a way to acknowledge these forces and maybe even ask for forgiveness. For I knew they had grown quite angry during their years unacknowledged. Through relating to them, perhaps I could lure them into daylight and discover their contributions.

But who were the Spider and the Hag? I knew their shadow side – their negativity and bitterness, and their power to paralyze. But what other kind of power lived hidden in this shadow? Did spiritual life really have a place for that power? I did not understand who these figures were beyond my frightened and frightening experience of them. I had to take a closer look.

Many winter mornings I sat at the computer researching what was so often referred to as the "dark feminine." I read stories of goddesses of the underworld, ecstatic wise women with skulls around their necks dancing in the charnel grounds, and I read the story of a goddess revealing her vagina to soldiers to befuddle them and stop their fighting. None of it seemed relevant to my life. None of it made much sense to me.

I read that the dark feminine had to do with creation, the powers of creation, and the material world and all its mysteries. I could not conceptually understand what this meant, but I was moved by poems or descriptions of the spider as a creative force of life, spinning all creation from the darkness of her abdomen. Many of the references highlighted the aloneness of the spider, and always identified her as a feminine force. The Hopis imaged her as a goddess of creation:

"I am Kokyanwuhti," the Spider Woman crooned. "I receive Light and nourish Life. I am Mother of all that shall ever come."[13]

Some likened the Spider's creativity to the essential nature of the soul. I found a Walt Whitman poem that touched something deep inside me:

A noiseless, patient spider,
I mark'd, where, on a little promontory, it stood, isolated;
Mark'd how, to explore the vacant, vast surrounding,
It launch'd forth filament, filament, filament, out of itself;
Ever unreeling them – ever tirelessly speeding them.

And you, O my Soul, where you stand,

Surrounded, surrounded, in measureless oceans of space,
Ceaselessly musing, venturing, throwing,--seeking the spheres, to
* connect them;*
Till the bridge you will need, be form'd--till the ductile anchor
* hold;*
Till the gossamer thread you fling, catch somewhere, O my
* Soul.*

This soul work of the Spider was what I longed to come to know and live. The darkness as a creative force intrigued me. Did the Hag also hold secrets in her dark wooded home having to do with creation?

I had to come to know these dark forces, or there would be no life at all for me, just more hauntings from the past. The research was not really helping. I did not know where I could meet this energy, but I resolved to do whatever it took to find my own inner spider and hag. Even if it meant waiting a long time to meet her face to face.

Then I saw her.

And yes, she looked like a crone all right. Staggering out of the bedroom, in a groggy grumpiness. She was not pretty. She had hair all over, sticking out in funny places. She was big around the hips. She had breakfast stuck in her scraggly beard.

She was Pearlie.

Rejected, abandoned, disdained, left behind in the shadows for the light of Truth, like all the great crones of history. Oh, my Pearl.

I watched her lick around her bowl for any forgotten breakfast, find a bit of old rice that stuck to her beard, and turn back to bed.

I remembered that the peace I was beginning to experience had not come without a price. Like those men on the hiking trail frustrated by Pearlie's ignorant slowness, a great frustration and anxiety had arisen in me, not so different than the anxiety I felt in my spider dreams. And being with Pearlie evoked the humiliation of being ordinary and useless. Like the crone, Pearlie had no place of prominence in the outer world. Pearlie had no dignity or pride or worldly beauty. She wasn't doing important spiritual work!

If I were to really be with her, I would be just like her. I would become slow and dense. And I would be alone, for the crone lived in her wooded hut, reviled by normal society.

It was her aloneness that terrified me most. My love for Pearlie allowed no separation, no sense of "other." In that love, there were no relationships. I was not with my teacher,; I had no outer place of belonging. There, I was on my own. I supposed that aloneness had to do with the aloneness of the Spider and the aloneness of the Crone. She was alone because she was rejected. But she was also alone because that was her nature.

There were prices to pay for Pearlie's secrets. If I wanted to know what creative feminine power is, the first step was to accept my outer and inner aloneness and my own humility and let go of any kind of outer assurances and reference points. For in Pearlie's world, there was no teacher, no path, no enlightenment. Just a strange presence of peace and wholeness hidden from the eyes of this world behind the veils of uselessness.

I had the sense, right then as Pearlie fell back into her bed with her usual harrumph, that power – real power – was in a place deep inside that was so alone it was completely free. I could see why no one would want to take that step; I could see why the King rejected the crone at the christening of his sweet Princess. Worldly power structures and securities did not exist in that realm of freedom. That was a place of complete surrender, where everything falls away except that which is real within one's being. If I could surrender into the freedom and vulnerability of *being* itself, maybe then Pearlie could lead me into those hidden places – like the spider's abdomen – where the multiplicity of life streams into existence like one strange silky string woven from within a deeper darkness.

Communion

*I am standing near a swamp or marsh. It is teeming with life.
Steam rises from black water. Reeds and grasses grow up from
the blackness, and small trees too. In the middle of the swamp
there is a clump of grasses, and two large snakes rise from the
green. They are twisted around each other, their heads facing
each other, their tongues flickering.*

*I stand transfixed. I am mesmerized by this mysterious beauty
and I want to get closer. I approach the swamp. I look deep
into the blackness of the water, moving closer and closer till my
head is over the darkness, looking down into the depths.*

*At first, my focus is lost and I only see darkness. But suddenly,
a seal breaks through the surface of the water, its black eyes
look straight into mine. It rises up to my face, kisses me on my
left cheek, and sinks slowly back down into the swamp.*

Perfection

In September, Mary the vet had given Pearlie three to six months to live. Now it was January and I expected Pearlie would not be with me much longer.

Pearlie's kind of cancer was most likely to spread first to her lungs and then to her other organs. I scheduled a chest x-ray to reveal how much the cancer had spread. I had felt so much pressure those previous months to learn from Pearlie, that her impending death symbolized a place of relief. I would miss her, but more strongly I longed for a time when I would feel less overwhelmed by both her presence and my resistance to her.

But Mary did not call to tell me where the cancer had spread. She called to tell me that there was no sign of cancer anywhere in Pearlie's body. "Pearlie's a "miracle dog!" she said with relief and excitement. She went on to explain that Pearlie's blood-work and x-rays showed a healthy nine-year old dog.

I hung up the phone, sat down on my yellow couch and stared at the rain coming down on the dark wood of my deck. Pearlie came out of the bedroom for a moment, and without concern for Mary's news, went right back to her bed. I tucked my legs under me and sighed.

Her recovery meant that I had more to learn from her. I was not going to say goodbye to Pearlie with mild appreciation of something new and beautiful, and a bewildered surrender to sadness.

And Pearlie? She was clearly not tired. In fact she was healthier than ever. She even seemed a bit smug those days. Maybe she knew she was example of God's infinite power and compassion. She still had that haunting sadness in her eyes, but she had more energy and excitement as well. Even other people noticed how she had changed, pointing out a renewed vigor. I saw it too, along with her growing sense of humor.

I watched the rain a while. I rested my head back against my scratchy kilim pillow and shut my eyes. I must have fallen asleep for a moment, and when I awoke Pearlie was back – right there by the couch. I didn't know what she wanted, but her big eyes seemed to be waiting for something. I bent down and touched her nose with my nose, squishing into that coolness, and she did not pull away. I pushed a little harder and her tongue flickered out and licked my upper lip before she shook her head and looked at me, again, waiting.

I laughed at her and myself, and got out my raincoat. I opened the door and we both moseyed up the dark and slippery streets with no particular agenda. It was quiet outside, everything shining in the water, Pearlie's paws making their momentary ripples of reflected streetlamps where the puddles were deep. The fresh air moist with rain bathed my face and rinsed away some tiredness. We walked slowly on for almost an hour. When we returned we both went to sleep.

Pearlie had been saved. I smiled at this unexpected development. But the really funny thing was that she was the miracle and I was still the same old me.

Spiritual life was bewildering. I could feel so much power and beauty in Pearlie and also in my direct perception of her. At times it was as though I could open a door and step into a joyful celebration full of light and love all contained in peace. So much belonging and joy! This celebration was complete perfection, just as I had experienced so many years before at camp. There was no need for anything else; a state of presence full of possibility and yet perfect as is. All creation alive and dancing in love!

And yet, unlike when I was a child, now I felt somehow separate. Just as it was Pearlie who was given new life, not me, the celebration was oddly remote. I could see and feel an eternal glory, like a party that had been going on since before time. But sadly I could not enjoy the party for long without wondering why I had never been invited.

What a strange paradox this was – to experience creation filled with so much divine presence, and at times resting and melting into its wholeness, and yet still feel so useless and left out. What was the point of me? Where was my place in this eternal joy?

I was caught in this unsettling no-man's land between my Self and my ego for quite a while. I could look back and forth – seeing this new peace and joy, and feeling saturated by it, but also seeing its complete "otherness," its total irrelevance to anything concerning my small self. That beautiful peace, slow moving and luring me into heavy communion, had no answers for my loneliness or sadness. That joyful sweetness and celebration were not solutions to the difficulties of my personality The "I" that was sad and lonely would never be helped, and certainly would never be enlightened.

My teacher used to quote the old Zen masters who described waking up to the joke of spiritual life. With glee, my teacher would explain that one day the seeker sees how absurd spiritual life is, and how misguided he has been. In fact, he sees right through projections, hopes and fantasies, and recognizes that there is no such thing as spiritual life at all. The "I" that searched and searched does not exist. The "I" can never be enlightened, for it was an illusion all along. In my case, there was no spiritual accomplishment, just a healthier and happier dog.

But I was confused. What was the purpose of the perception that remains? What should I do with this awareness of divine wholeness, which seemed to be so far away and also so near, part of the world beyond me and part of my own Self?

One afternoon after meditation at the center, I told my teacher of my frustration. I told him I could not fathom my part in this peace that has been present since before time. He tried to assure me that I was needed in this divine play – that my experience of presence was my way of participating. "By witnessing the perfection of creation, we see God here in His world," he explained, leaning against the kitchen wall of the retreat center. "We do this for Him," he said softly. "This is our contribution and our way to be in service."

I believed him, for this is how it felt. When I was in this state of being in which all things were whole in peace, I saw with eyes that were not my normal eyes. They saw love from a place of love; they saw light with a shared light. In that space I was present as watcher and participant both, in the same mysterious way that Pearlie seemed always to be offering me something new and waiting for me to receive it so we could simply be together.

Drowning in jewels

It was not long before spring came and budding was everywhere, and a new calmness had descended for which I was grateful. When frustration came, it seemed less jarring. And my sadness could sometimes be held away by even a slight smell of rain dampening the yard.

I sat at my desk one morning looking out my windows at clouds streaming on a wind across the hills. A blue jay came and landed on the deck, and squawked for food. I found some birdseed from my back cupboard, and piled it on the railing of the deck.

I watched the jay eat and I watched the pair of red-headed woodpeckers, who frequented one of my trees, come over and force the jay away. I heard an osprey cry from farther up in the fir trees. It was spring. My doubts, my confusion and sadness, had no bearing on spring's arrival.

I looked at Pearlie drinking her water, and I knew she would soon want to be let outside, one door or another. Spring was like Pearlie, entirely unconcerned with my changing mood. It was all around me, this lack of concern for me. Pearlie was like life, like spring, like my own soul, growing healthier and happier, more full of divine celebration and totally unconcerned by my ego's mood.

I felt chilled, like it had been such a long winter. But this spring was something new. Its warmth was a new warmth. I felt hopeful and awake, as if I was sitting on the edge of the world, watching a strange and beautiful storm cloud coming towards the land. It was raining diamonds and emeralds. It was raining so hard I thought I might drown in jewels.

That afternoon, just after lunch and Pearlie's walk, I had the sudden feeling to go away for a while with Pearlie. Spring was enticing me into itself, and I imagined Pearlie could enter that spring too and become saturated with its promises of newness and light.

I thought about a road trip up to Seattle, to stay with my cousins or nearby on Whidbey Island with a friend. It was hard to decide where to go. But eventually I thought a longer trip would be good. So I considered the small Connecticut town on Long Island Sound where my family has had a summer-house for a hundred years. Pearlie could wade in the salt water, wander our quiet pebbled roads without fear of traffic, and roll in the grasses of one yard after another, returning home when she felt like it.

I thought six weeks was enough time to drive cross-country, write for a while, and drive home. And more importantly, it seemed enough time to be alone with Pearlie, far from my teacher. I wanted to revel in this space where life was simple and gentle and so alive, and see what could grow from within that life.

I told my teacher about my plans, and he confirmed that it was a good idea. He laughed and made it seem fun – Pearlie and me on the road. His confirmation was nice to hear, and I was happy at the possibility of this joy he hinted at.

About a week after my teacher and I talked about the trip, he ended an afternoon meditation and called out my name. I looked up, and he said I should leave for six months, not six weeks. I was shocked. He continued, saying it was time for me to claim something, and I could only do it away from him.

At the time I did not really understand what he meant, but I watched his face become soft and caring. "You love me too much," he said as he rested his head against the back wall and gently closed his eyes.

I felt then in the silence of that moment how heavy sadness and love both were, and how sometimes they flowed in and out of each other so I could not tell the difference.

Six months was a long time. But if I was still so drawn to him, so attached to him and to the energy that came through him that I could not really give myself to Pearlie, then I needed to be gone. After all, I reminded myself, I would return once something was complete. Six months was not forever.

And I knew he was right. How could I fully come into my own being when I loved someone who was so completely absorbed in the nothingness of non-existence? He had been made empty so many years ago during his spiritual training. His training, like those of the greatest saints, had allowed hardly any human qualities to remain. He was like those dervishes described by Rumi, "…*there is no dervish in the world; or if there be, that dervish is really not there.*" [14]

And I, in my love for him, was drawn into the space where he was not. It's not as mysterious as it sounds. It's as though you are sitting on a hill in a warm evening watching the sky fill with sunset colors. When the sun drops into that little pocket behind the horizon line, a small bit of you goes with it into the magnificent darkness you sense just behind the edge of the world. And walking home, you can even sense that missing piece, now absorbed into the new night that is all around.

That's how it was for me, every evening after meditating with him. A little of me was gone into that swirling darkness beyond. Unfortunately every morning, that distant piece was right back in place.

I had to accept that I was not allowed to disappear like that. I had to come to terms with being fully here, in this world. Maybe I secretly hoped I could skip the "here" part and go right into the beyond. Maybe that was why those Buddhist practices had never worked for me. It seemed there was a whole aspect of being "here" that had to be included before I could experience the beyond.

I remembered, years earlier, visiting with a shaman from West Africa. She said something that had surprised me and always stayed with me. She explained that it was through relating to the Earth that one could journey into realms beyond the earth.[15] One did not find other dimensions by rejecting this dimension, she had told me.

I had the feeling she was right, that something of the nothing-ness of non-being could not be experienced until I had surren-dered into being.

I had many things to do before I left. A whole month went by, during which nothing happened but preparations for the trip. I made lots of CDs to listen to along the way. I made sure Pearlie had all her shots and enough food and snacks for six months. I cleaned my house so the person who would sublet it could move into a clean and fairly empty space. I hoped he would bond a bit with my cat.

My teacher did not speak to me during this time. In fact, he seemed particularly cold and distant. One day I almost ran into him in the parking lot after meditation and he looked quickly away from me as though I wasn't there. I asked him why he was ignoring me and he said with such coldness, "I'm done with you now," and walked on.

It was hard for me to feel his coldness. But I assumed he was making sure I could leave simply, with no emotional ties or re-grets. There was really nothing left for me there. Even my editing work for him was over; he had given me nothing to work on for weeks. I tried to follow his hints, and let my own coldness play its part ensuring a clean and unemotional departure so that when the time came, Pearlie and I could drive away and not look back.

The Heart Sutra

There were things I needed for my time away. Soon after I began to plan my trip, I acquired something I had had no idea I needed. I dreamt:

> *I am in a store. The store is dark, and many of the items in the store are beautiful old antiques. I look for a long time at small old black objects. Then I move to another part of the store, and I open a closet. Sitting on a shelf of the closet are two giant bright red apples.*

> *I lift one apple and take a bite. The sweetness is beyond anything I could imagine. My mouth comes alive! Pure sweetness coats my mouth and throat, and is absorbed deep into my body, which receives it ecstatically.*

> *Next to the apples sits a tape recorder with headphones. I put the headphones on and listen to the tape. The music I hear is as though from Heaven. It is music from another world. So beautiful! Like nothing I have ever heard.*

> *I take the tape up to the counter to buy it. I look down at the tape, and I see written on the label, the title of the music. I am surprised to see that it is called "The Heart Sutra."*

> *The saleswoman looks down at the tape, and up at me, and says, in a questioning voice, "Buying a belief today?"*

If there was a belief I needed, if there was a belief that would help me in my surrender to my love for Pearlie and to life itself, it was a belief in the fundamental Buddhist teaching of the Heart Sutra – Prajnaparamita. Prajnaparamita, the wisdom of emptiness, reveals that all things are empty of independent reality, and yet all things are interdependent. It reads:

> *"Form is emptiness; emptiness also is form. Emptiness is no other than form; form is no other than emptiness. In the same way, feeling, perception, formation, and consciousness are emptiness.... There is no decrease and no increase...no ignorance, no end of ignorance up to no old age and death, no end of old age and death; no suffering, no origin of suffering, no cessation of suffering, no path, no wisdom, no attainment, and no non-attainment."*[16]

A paradox confusing to the mind, Prajnaparamita struck me in the depths of my being. I knew this understanding lived inside of me. I knew its teachings on the essential emptiness of all forms and the essential *isness* of emptiness was Pearlie's teaching, for in my love for Pearlie, emptiness and form flowed back and forth revealing a presence that was at the same time both yet neither.

I had been so mistaken those earlier years doing my Buddhist practices when I thought emptiness was somewhere else. I don't know where my teacher's non-existence is or is not. But my dream shows that emptiness is somehow here and not here.

Pearlie was such a good example of this mystery. She was, of course, a living being. And yet she was characterized most by the odd and haunting sense that something was missing. She was so much not a normal dog! She was so still, so simple, so undistinguishable – like space. In Pearlie's presence there were no attachments, no goals. There was nothing. But in that nothing love came forth with endless laughter.

Believing in the Heart Sutra would help me let go of my striving and my attachments and rest in my love for Pearlie. And this love was slowly drawing me toward my Self, what the Alchemists call the *Pearl of Great Price*, the divine source manifest within the human being. I knew my love for Pearlie was taking me within, to my Self, for the feelings she evoked were vast and impersonal, limitless and free, so far beyond my ego's restrictions. The peace, love and presence she awoke in me were near, but had nothing to do with me. They belonged to the realm of my soul, they belonged to the divine within.

From that place of being, I could play my part in how love and light flow from the formless nothingness into the magnificence of manifestation. Like the breath, back and forth, here and there, in and out, again and again and again...

I let myself believe that it was possible that the emptiness of God was here in life – in me! – as well as deep in the beyond. I gently let believing itself pull me into the warmth of its company I let it assure me that something of life could taste like that apple, sweet beyond anything I had tasted, reaching senses I had no idea existed.

I let myself believe that it was all possible. And it was.

But first, I had to leave the garden.

3

Back east

Both bliss and gried you have been to me,
But of woe far greater hath been my share.
You were caught away from all perils free,
But my pearl was gone, I knew not where;
My sorrow is softened now I it see

The Pearl Poet

On the road

Early morning late in August after a long sunrise run in the hills behind my house and breakfast with Roger on his porch looking over the bay, Pearlie and I left everything behind but each other.

As we pulled out of town, I remembered how simple my teacher made it sound. I just needed to be away for a while so something new could come into being. "It will be interesting to see what comes into that space!" he had said with a sparkle, referring to the space of freedom and openness I had begun to feel. What was coming? I wondered and was so eager for whatever it was – something new, something challenging, something to draw me deeper into life or myself – I hoped.

On the road I just drove and drove. I barely noticed the scenery. I did not care which towns I was passing through. I just drove.

From that first day, I only remember that California and Nevada were so hot. I had covered all the car windows in the back with "baby shades" but despite the plastic coatings, Pearlie was hot and agitated. She managed to pace in the small space of the car. And she looked at me again and again, as though pleading with me to relieve her anxiety. Her discomfort made me anxious. I went back and forth between having the air conditioner turned off and the windows down for fresh air, and then the windows up and air conditioner on, for coolness that I was always worried would not reach the back seat.

Late that first night we reached Salt Lake City. I had been tempted to stop earlier to sleep, but I could not stomach Nevada's casino billboards that advertised gambling and women with low tops and short skirts. It was a relief, a deep and potent change, to enter the Mormon state where even coffee is a rarity.

In the motel in Salt Lake, Pearlie acted strangely. Neither of us could sleep. She paced from one end of the room to the other for hours. Eventually, and very uncharacteristically, she wanted to come onto the bed. There, she panted with nervousness as she looked to me for reassurance.

Finally she could relax, late in the night, with me slowly petting her belly and side. She would put her head down, close her eyes, and start to breathe more deeply. But as soon as her breathing really evened out, just when it seemed she was asleep, she would startle awake again, lift her head, open her eyes wide, and we would start the whole nervous process again.

We hardly slept at all – maybe two hours – and I was worried about Pearlie and scared to drive on so little sleep. But we did make it to Boulder the next day, where we stayed with an old friend, and her new little shepherd mix.

Even after three days of rest, Pearlie and I were stiff and anxious. My body was not having an easy time with the drive, and my back hurt significantly. I was worried about more driving. At least the sky was overcast and the air was cool on the day we left Boulder. Pearlie would not have to suffer in such heat.

On the way out of town, I stopped at the supermarket to get a sandwich and some supplies for the long drive through Nebraska. I opened my door in the parking lot, and almost ran into a man with a small dog walking right by my car. I was taken aback by their immediate presence. Then I thought I recognized the man from somewhere, some other time. I looked at him, but in my usual unwillingness to engage with strangers turned toward the market. As I was walking away I heard him call my name. I stopped, turned back around and said, while trying to discern who he was, "Yes. What's your name?" It was James, from my psychology program at the Buddhist school in Boulder, more than seven years earlier.

In the moment that I said hello, I wondered why I was running into him. I told him I was on my way through Nebraska and that it was such a coincidence to see him. He explained that he had become a massage therapist, and had a chair set up near the entrance of the market. He was just taking his dog for a walk, but insisted on giving me a massage.

At first I hesitated – I don't like massages from people I didn't know very well. But I was in awe of this coincidence. And Pearlie was safe in a shady parking spot. I was still very sore, so I agreed.

I sat on the chair, and felt myself immediately relax into his touch. At first, I began to feel a bit sick. I felt heavy and queasy. But soon I felt calmer and more grounded. I thanked him so much. I bought my snacks, and we drove away.

I felt given to, and I was very grateful.

Somewhere between Nebraska and Iowa, when even Pearlie began to feel a bit more relaxed, I pulled into a rest stop to use the bathroom, give Pearlie water, and walk her a bit. As I was driving away, I passed by the truck parking area, and I noticed a huge eighteen-wheeler pulling out alongside me. A single advertisement was blazoned across its side. There was a picture of a sword cutting across the entire length of the truck, and large words, said, "Always Earned. Never Given." It was an advertisement for the U.S. Marines.

How difficult it is, I thought, to live in a culture that only believes in earning. I thought of that mysterious passage in the Bible, when Christ says to his disciples,

> *Peace I leave with you, my peace I give unto you: not as the world giveth, give I unto you…*[17]

This passage hints at the gifts of grace, how what is divine comes freely, not by effort or willpower, not by the rules of this world. Peace, I had come to know, existed beyond striving.

I watched the truck pass out of view and felt glad not to have that giant sword staring down at me. I whispered to myself and to Pearlie in the back of the car, "The world fights and earns but the gifts of God are free."

Incident at Warren Dunes

Michigan was beautiful. The green flowed in from Iowa, but there was more water in this state – more lakes and rivers. I felt myself breathe easier within the kaleidoscope of dark earth, vivid green fields, and all the flowing waterways.

There were state parks everywhere with lakeside motels and access to Lake Michigan beaches, and Pearlie and I stopped at one of the parks called "Warren Dunes." It was hot in the car, and I thought we might be able to wade in the water, the way Pearlie liked. Soon we would be at a retreat center where we would be staying for a few days, and I wanted to be out of the car with Pearlie before we had to be with people.

It had been raining all morning, but the weather was clearing a bit. The sun was seeping through the cloud cover with tenderness, the rain seemed subdued into a foggy haze. The lake was vast and clear, and the beach was soft sand, spreading out for miles and miles. Pearlie and I were so glad to be out of the car. She seemed especially energetic, and we ran together for a while.

We approached a small family swimming in the water. Their young daughter, maybe seven years old, brightened at the sight of Pearlie and came up to pet her. Then we walked on for about half an hour in the warm wet air. Pearlie would run a bit, and then go into the lake, walking slowly through the water as it flowed by her legs and belly.

At one point Pearlie went into the water and stood quite a while, enjoying the waves moving beneath her. But then she took a step, and it must have been off a shelf in the sand. I could see her lose her footing a bit. At first it was just a slow sinking outwards, away from the water's edge. I laughed to myself, because I knew I would be seeing something I had never seen before – Pearlie swimming! She had never gone into deep water back home.

But there was no swimming. She just let herself slip down – slip away. First she floated a bit. Her face was totally expressionless. She could have been curious about what was happening, or maybe she even liked how the water now surrounded her – the water now all over her, as a soothing pressure.

Then she began to sink. First her back, then her head went under. She made no effort to stay above water. She made no attempt to swim. She just sank. So softly, so gently, like a strange dream. Like a cloud dissolving into the sky.

I could not believe what was happening. I quickly kicked off my sandals and shook off my coat and jumped into the water. It was deeper than I thought, well above my waist. I struggled to grab Pearlie under her stomach and I pulled her up to the sand.

She had not swallowed any water. She lay on the sand for a moment, looking confused, as though trying to adjust to where she was. She made eye contact with me, and I tried to look excited instead of scared, as though she had just had a fun adventure. She caught that look, got up and shook herself off, and began to wander back to the car. Then she changed her pace to a run, shaking off the experience as she stopped to shake the water from her coat – again and again until she just ran on seemingly without memory.

Driving north, I could not get the scene out of my head. What kind of a creature was she? Letting herself just sink away? Later on the drive, still disturbed, I called Nan. She was out, so I talked to Roger. I told him what had happened, I told him how strange it was to watch Pearlie let herself drown.

Roger said to me, based on his experience in a war decades earlier, "It can be very disturbing watching someone surrender."

Pearlie might be surrendered, allowing things to happen as they will, with no struggle. But it was not her time to go. It was not her time to sink back down into the ocean before time. We still had things to do, and I still needed her help. I tried to put the scene behind me as we drove on to our next destination, but I remained distracted by Pearlie's near drowning. I just wanted to be alone with her on solid ground, to stroke her and hold her, and claim her back to this world with my love.

On the Sound

After a few more days driving, Pearlie and I arrived in Connecticut. I was finally home at our house on Long Island Sound.

The Sound itself was calm on the day we arrived, and marked by a few ships and a strip of land on the horizon – Long Island, five miles away. I drove through the quiet stone roads past one soft green lawn after another. Garden flowers were still in bloom against the wide gray walls of the shingled cottages, climbing up the white fences and porch railings.

Children ran around through the yards and beaches, mostly in their pink and white and navy blue. I passed the tennis courts, which were busy with Labor Day contests. I arrived with the ice cream truck, which rang its sing-song bells behind me until the children blocked its way with their dollar bills and hungry smiles.

I pulled up to our family home, a renovated barn facing the waters of the Sound. The barn was next to the big house – my grandmother's family house – where I spent childhood summers when I was not at camp. Now my aunt and uncle lived there.

My mother had been staying in our cottage off and on during the summer with her grandchildren, my brother's two sons. She and my stepfather lived nearby, and she would move back into their house at summer's end.

I was happy to be home. Something in me relaxed deeply. It was partly just the end of driving, the end of being anxious in the car and worried about Pearlie. It was also something deeper. I could relax here. Our little town was a welcome change from the intensity and discomfort of my life in California.

Here, many of us were related, old Connecticut families, cousins of cousins, familiar and comforting. Everyone drove golf carts around because the community was so private, few cars came and went.

All day long large tankers would line up off the coast to wait their turn to head up the Connecticut River. After dinner people would stroll down by the sea wall, stop in at a neighbor's cottage, interrupting dinner or cocktails to say hello to relatives and friends.

The swans were still in the cove. Bright and fishing by day, safe under their wings at night or in the light rain. The U.S. Open was on TV, and my mother and I watched for hours. At night, the green light of the lighthouse cut across the black sky over and over again.

Pearlie was happy. She loved being in Connecticut. She seemed to understand right away that the whole community was hers. There were few fences, just endless grass. She would amble around outside on the lawns and on the pebbled roads, and down the seawall onto the beach. I let her go, and just trusted that she knew to come back. She had never lived somewhere without a fence, and I loved imagining how happy she was to wander as far as she wanted.

Life was simple here. The first month or so my inner life virtually disappeared. I didn't dream much, and my meditation was simple but a bit dull. I didn't mind this decrease in inner activity. There were so many times in the preceding months when I felt exhausted by my dreams and worn out by trying to understand what to do or how to do it.

Pearlie loved the grass. She rolled in it almost every day. We had no thick green grass in California. Here, I could only assume that it felt good to her, so thick and cool against her belly, her head and back.

We had a favorite new game. I would let Pearlie out of the house, and she would wander off. After about a half hour, I would start to worry. Where was she? Was she alright? Did she know how to get home? I would spend another ten or fifteen minutes letting go of my anxiety, finding a place where I trusted that everything was OK.

And then, when I felt it was out of genuine concern rather than panicky need, I would get on my old blue three-speed Schwinn bike and look for her. I would head out to the sea wall and go right, first, checking all the yards down to the pier. Then I would turn back up by the golf course and home again.

It was like being on an Easter egg hunt. I would look through the hedges, along the yards, behind the houses, until I would see that soft white vision moving ghost-like and in such high contrast against the green grass or slate-gray shingles or dusky skies. In her own world, going her own pace, I would watch for a while, from a distance. But I could not hold back for long. I would approach, and this was the great moment. Pearlie would notice me, and it was like she hadn't seen me in a million years. It was like she had so completely forgotten me that my presence was a total surprise.

Or, maybe it was that she feared herself to be lost, but when she saw me she was flooded with the feeling of having been found.

She would jump up, then put her head down, run at me, and then run on. Then, suddenly as the excitement came, she would return to a slow ambling, sniffing here and there, as though lost again in a completely new forgetting.

The game reminded me of something my mother and stepfather do in the summer. As the day ends, and the light begins to disappear, they go out strolling down the edge of the golf course where the grasses grow tall, looking for golf balls. I remember in the years before that they encouraged me to come along, but I was bored even thinking about it. My mother was surprised that I didn't find it exciting, the way the light caught the white balls so they shone in the tall grass, the thrill of finding one glowing in the shadows, carrying it home like a trophy. I never did. But things had changed, and now I understood.

The glow of the pearl

Weeks after we arrived, Pearlie seemed so calm. She rolled in the grass; she liked her walks. She loved the shoreline wind. She didn't seem to want much from me. Sometimes I would pet her, and she would subtly move away. I felt her become more and more independent, and the worry I used to feel for her disappeared. Since finding her in the shelter, I had hoped to relieve her sadness, that emptiness I saw in her eyes. I never had been able to make her a happy dog. But now I no longer felt burdened by her incapacity to be happy. She seemed fine on her own, and her independence released me from a place of inner anxiety, which had been present for many years.

In the mornings, when I worked at the kitchen table, she would come out of the bedroom looking bedraggled and sleepy. I would greet her excitedly, and she would step near. At times she let me pet her, but other times she would veer off, slightly, so as to avoid me on the way to her water bowl. She made me laugh when she would stop, just out of my reach, forcing me to get out of the chair, proving my affection. She still had her sense of humor, and she just seemed content.

And so was I. In the afternoon, after writing and going for a run, I spent a lot of time lying in the grass, either outside my house or down by the pier. It was so quiet! The gulls, the wind, a lawnmower far way, a bicycle wheel on gravel every now and then. Not much else.

In California my house was above a busy street. It was never quiet. There was no outdoor space for me. Back East, I loved being outside – walking, lying, hearing so many sounds, tiny against all the vastness.

Sometimes I wondered where this new "thing" was that my teacher indicated would come into the space of freedom that had grown in recent months. I wanted something to come and draw me into a new world, a new engagement with life. Nothing came, though, and I tried to leave concern in the background, behind all the sounds of late summer. Mostly I felt simple, like Pearlie. There was no time, and no urgencies related to time. Everything was beautiful and whispery.

And what was this kindness I sensed?

It seemed as though the sky was kind to the tree-tops, the birds were kind to the branches. The light was kind to the reeds in the wind, which reflected the light's gifts as splashes of kindness to the breeze.

It is was though all the creation spoke to itself in kindness.

And those late afternoons lying on the grass looking up – what a wonder it was to see the gulls flying home at the end of the day, their bodies now higher then the sinking sun, underlit and glowing with that pale pink of sunset, as though they each had a small Christmas light hidden in their breast.

I did not need to feel the dramatic or ecstatic love that I had felt in California. The peace that started to saturate my days seemed more natural, more a part of my stream of experience rather than a contrasting event. It grew inside me and outside me at the same time.

And sometimes, deeper than the peace, I felt the presence of a hidden power. During these moments I felt like a plant, or a piece of fruit, with hidden inner cells multiplying exponentially, expanding into infinity, and at the same time remaining just as I was and always had been. This power was sometimes so gentle, other times furiously expanding, and seemed like something giving birth to itself continuously and yet not changing.

I recognized this peace and power with great respect. I felt as though life itself was telling me everything was OK and it wanted to me to come closer. It was an invitation I had been longing for, promises of new life and new depths of experience.

One evening, when I was lying in my little twin bed with the mahogany posts in the room behind the kitchen, I was feeling so grateful for Pearlie and the places she had taken me. I got out of bed and went over to where she lay at the foot of the other twin bed, and I stroked her head. I thanked her for helping me, and I asked if she would help me more, if she would help me come closer to her and these secrets our love unveiled.

Now usually Pearlie was not a very attentive girl. But while I stroked her ears, she looked at me with an intelligence and attention I had not seen before. And in that moment I was surprised to feel that she understood what I was asking. I was interested to see if something would change the next day.

Something did change.

That next day and for a few days following, Pearlie closed her eyes. It was too distinct not to notice, and I had to assume that this was what she was showing me. I would call her over, and she would approach, and then slowly she would shut her eyes and stand in front of me. And when she was lying down, when I came near, she would just keep her eyes shut, even while I pet her. Usually she would look at me when I came over, assessing what I wanted or what I was doing. But not now.

So, I took her cue and closed my eyes. Not literally, but inwardly. I subdued an inner drive to look, search, or find. I stopped assuming there was anything to see. I stopped worrying about what was coming or not coming. Instead of looking up and outward, I turned my eyes down, into darkness. It was such a subtle but significant difference, like the difference between praying to something "out there," giving myself to something "other" than myself, and prayer to the inner, to what is within, already present.

Turning inward there was space, and also more. Always looking out, up, hoping for confirmation or reflection from beyond
myself, had made me tired and expectant. Looking inward was
more like Pearlie. Things there just are.

In moments, it felt like I was sinking slowly downward, and
then gently starting to unfurl.

And there was a new delicacy to the peace I had been feeling.
Like how a scent is, just at the tips of a flower. Or how it feels
when a breeze is just at its beginning – the slightest and earliest
of movements. At times I felt like a bird carried down from the
mountains on a river of wind into the sweetness of wildflowers
below.

I wouldn't be looking outward again. Not for a while. I made a
promise to myself to relax into what is present inside, even if the
darkness was unnerving. For as peaceful as it was, this darkness
was also frightening. I felt a disturbing powerless in letting go of
outer prayer, letting go of trying to please God, please my teacher.
I remembered, again, how Pearlie had never seemed particularly
interested in knowing or doing what I wanted. I even needed to
let go of my old interest in doing what is right.

Without my usual focus, I was left weak and vulnerable. I felt
afraid. I recognized the vulnerability of surrender. But what was I
surrendering to? In that darkness there was no teacher, no outer
power. There was only a weakness and unknowing. It was a place
to live from, moment to moment, if I could bear that degree of
vulnerability.

It emanated a beauty, a soft light.

I recognized this light. It was Pearlie's light. A full moon of a
pearl. It was a light that did not shine in any direction. It was not
like a flashlight. And it was not like the sun, which cast a shadow.
It was all around and luminous, as though glowing from within
everything.

All life had a light inside. It was the light of being in love with God. And it was everywhere.

Pearlie went outside that night to wander around, and she did not come back for an hour. I was certain she was just doing her usual routine – moseying around people's yards, sniffing bushes at her pleasure. But it was a weekend, and some people had returned so there were a few cars. I was worried. Pearlie did not understand cars, nor could she see or hear them well. So I went out on my bicycle in the early darkness to find her.

I rode down the streets a bit, and then back to the house and out to the sea wall. I wanted to make sure she was not down by the water, caught between the waves and the concrete. I reached the wall, and looked down.

There, exactly beneath where I stood, a young boy sat on the sand. He was maybe nine years old. He sat on his knees, leaning above a fish – a blue fish I assumed – which was still caught on the end of a line attached to a rod. He was bashing the fish with a rock. He was hitting it again and again, on the head, on its soft body. Then, he dropped the rock and raised his fists, and punched it, the blood dirtying his fist. A younger girl sat nearby, with the rod in her hands, just watching. The boy suddenly sensed my presence and looked up.

His face reflected an unnerving mix of desperation and raw need. He asked me, as though pleading with me, "Is it dead yet?"

I said I didn't know, and I rode off.

Riding away down the sidewalk, my bare feet pinched slightly by the plastic peddles, I knew I should not have gone out to look for Pearlie. I knew that too much looking just brought up a desperation like the feelings I saw on the boy's face, and in his pounding fist. Pearlie, and the real Pearl, did not need to be sought after. They waited in a place of silence and rest, where looking only takes you away.

Belly dancing

Becoming aware of this soft inner light within life was a first step. But another step followed: bringing that light outward, so that inner light could flow into a dance of creation. I was shown something of this dance as summer began to turn to fall. I dreamed:

I am with a large gathering or party, which includes friends from California and my teacher, though I didn't see him. Alison, a friend from the Sufi group, is there, and she wants to do a belly dance.

Alison enters to the middle of the group and starts dancing. Her hips move back and forth, her arms swirl above her head; she flows beautifully through the space.

Suddenly, after a quick move of her hips, there are two of her dancing, and then three, and four, five and finally six. Six Alisons dance in bright costumes, bells jangling on their hips, in constantly changing patterns, their dark hair thrown this way and that.

When she is finished, I tell her how amazing her dancing was, and ask her how she did it. She explains that it is easy! – She says she learned only in the ten minutes before she began.

"I just throw myself outward from my belly," She says. "Until there enough of myself to dance with."

A magic dance was taking place. Something from deep within my friend's belly was thrown out into life, where it came alive into its own swirling, flowing being.

The dream was symbolic of something I had longed to know. It was feminine power in its creative form – life pouring from the belly to create new life and a magical dance, like Grandmother spider spinning creation from herself.

Dreams contain few casual details, and I knew it was not irrelevant that by the end of the dream there were six Alisons. I had learned from years of listening to others' dreams, that six often represents a union of opposites. Six is the number of bringing heaven and earth together, the above and below. The six-pointed Star of David is created by two triangles – one which points above and one which points below. This is the union of masculine energy, driving upwards, and feminine energy, descending downwards, and the realization of the Alchemical mystery of oneness, "As above, so below."

I awoke that morning in awe. I knew I had witnessed something beautiful and powerful. Somewhere, far away, a dance was beginning. An inner power within creation was flowing outward in a mysterious dance of oneness.

I jumped out of the covers and tried to squeeze myself into Pearlie's blue doughnut-shaped bed on the floor. I kissed her ears and pushed my nose into her neck. She didn't know what the fuss was about and tried to pull away, but there was no more space. She looked at me and I laughed. "Something's coming Pearlie!" I almost yelled into her deaf ear. She pawed at my shoulder, edging her belly out from underneath her so I could pet it. I kissed her paw and smelled its glorious mustiness – a smell like no other – while I stroked the soft fur of her stomach. We lay there for a while, Pearlie going back to sleep while I thought about Alison.

Alison was a friend from my meditation group in California, but she had a full time job in the marketing division of a magazine company. She had a boyfriend. She was part of ordinary life.

I felt this meant that this dance needed outer, ordinary life in order to fully manifest. And I was yearning for this outer life. I was waiting for something new to come to me, as my teacher indicated. I was waiting for something to draw me into life and reflect this dance, which was already beginning in the inner worlds. But where was it? It was still a missing piece. So I waited and hoped. I stayed squeezed with Pearlie in her bed for a while longer. And throughout the week I kept close to her.

4

Dying

The lover is a king above all kings,
Unafraid of death, not at all
interested in a golden crown.
The dervish has a pearl concealed
under his patched cloak.
Why should he go begging door to door?[18]

Rumi

A moment

It always seems like there is one fall day or one particular storm that takes all the leaves from the trees. This day came, and suddenly the air was a flurry with color, and the carpeted ground was loud and crackling. The reds and golds swarming above were like burning angels or Tibetan nuns in high winds. These flying nuns of the new season were no black and white Sally Fields, but flaming cheeked Pema Wangchuks and Jigme Dolmas, their maroon robes and yellow under skirts flying across the sky like living invitations to a celestial mardi gras.

Since ours was a summer community, almost every house was now vacant. The large cottages stood on the edge of the shore like ships waiting to sail, their un-shuttered windows like open eyes scanning the horizon.

I felt at home with these ghostly houses. And a few people remained. A friend of my mother's and his beautiful pure-bred Samoyed, Czar the third (there had been other Czars, in the years before), lived three houses down to the left. Occasionally I would chat with him, while stopping to pet Czar. Sometimes Czar's owner's girlfriend would visit and bring her Siberian husky who would climb along the second floor porch to lie in his spot on the roof in the sun, like a panther.

An older woman, reclusive and quiet, lived next to Czar. I saw her only when she went out early to pick up her mail. I could hear her singing, occasionally, on her short and slow walk to the mailbox.

Duke's mom (Duke was a miniature poodle) lived five houses to the right. She loved Pearlie, and always commented on how energetic Pearlie seemed, compared to when we first arrived.

Pearlie didn't mind that she was not royalty like the other off-season dogs. She concentrated on the fall. The coldness energized her; the wind excited her. I loved the fall too, and the days went on, one after another, with hints of the sharp newness only reflected by winter.

One day in late October the winds settled themselves slightly and my mother came over to play tennis. The sun was bright; the gentle breezes off the Sound were damp and cool. Rustling leaves scuttled across the tennis court. My mother wore white, for even off-season she dressed for the game. It was her birthday, and as a present I was playing tennis with her. My back and hips were still very sore from the drive – even months later – and maybe it wasn't so good for me to play. But she loved it so much, and we were laughing and both playing well.

There are moments in life where everything seems to fall away in an instant and reconfigure in brand new way. On the tennis courts that day, such a moment appeared, and changed everything.

It began when my mother went looking for a ball amongst the leaves at the back of the court. I heard the leaves rustling and saw the sun glaring off the bright metal fence. As she came back to the baseline to serve, I was wondering about how things had been going here, in Connecticut. I was wondering why, even here, there was still this feeling of nothing happening, nothing really changing. There seemed all the time in the world to consider why my life still felt empty and why I sometimes allowed my old grief to stake its claim into that emptiness. For I still found myself longing to be back in that old love and belonging I had felt those early years with my teacher.

As my mother slowly returned to the baseline with the ball in hand, a question came to mind, and I asked myself, "What kind of person do I want to be?" At first I felt only the vacancy that always revealed itself when I considered the future. There was no answer but an echoing nothingness. Like the empty sounds haunting the Marabar Caves in *A Passage to India*. *Wathomp*. *Wathomp*. Nothing but the boom of vacancy.

But another question unexpectedly arose, "What kind of person does Pearlie need me to be?" And even as my mother was beginning her service, as she stepped so carefully just to the edge of the white tape with her left foot, there was endless time to ponder this question. I saw myself back with my teacher, but there was nothing but sadness there, and I could not see Pearlie.

Then something in me stopped paying attention to that old sadness. And suddenly an answer emerged from those inner caves. This answer declared, as my mother raised her hand with that bright yellow ball and released it generously to the sky, "*I want to be a person who sees God everywhere!*"

I was stunned by this answer. I was stunned by the presence of any answer at all from a space I thought would always be empty. But I did not deny it, and I saw what I truly wanted, and what I had always wanted.

I immediately felt the impact of this revelation, as though an order had been given and an inner army of troops had re-aligned. Sounds like flags unfurling, canvas snapping into the wind, filled my head. The world shifted, and I faced a direction I had never faced; I stood at the border of a landscape I had never entered.

This is what Pearlie had been waiting for. She needed me to know her. She was waiting for me to see her for who she was, created from the same love that tied my heart to my teacher, made from the love that turned my heart to God. But to know Pearlie meant to unknow everything else. To live fully from the place of oneness within meant the death of the "me" that had been the center of my life.

I played on, but I felt a storm approach. There was a thick and swirling void in front of me, and it was hard to stay steady. I had seen what I really wanted, and I knew there would be consequences to this recognition. I was weakened, and I stumbled and missed my mother's serve.

From deep inside this weakness came a demand for help. A prayer. This was the second emanation from those caves, now suddenly so generous after years of holding tight to their treasure. I could not do this on my own. I needed someone's hand to reach down and pull me toward where I was headed, for I had no idea how to get there myself, or even where it was.

I felt as deeply as I had ever felt anything that I had been heard and my prayers would be answered. Sometimes you just know. Something was coming. I would be given a way to leave everything behind and embrace something new. I did not know how or what was approaching. I just knew from my fear and anticipation that all would change.

We finished our game and soon the night fell slowly upon the Sound.

The moon rose, and then became a glowing red shadow, a luminous fireball in the lunar eclipse.

Later still, the Red Sox won the world-series, beating the curse that had been on them for so many years.

And the curse on Sleeping Beauty was over, and she woke up into a new day.

Resting in the pearl

*I am with my teacher and some others from our group, and I
am told that I will die soon; I am the next person of the group to
go. I am afraid, as though I know this death. Then I see mostly
darkness, and I struggle with fear, trying to stay calm in a limbo
state as one world recedes, fearing nothing new will come.*

All day, walking with Pearlie, writing, eating lunch, watching TV
after dinner, I wondered about this dream. Something was true
about it, and it had to do with the moment on the tennis court.

On the courts, something had been completed. I had said "Yes"
to a new life, and "Yes" to a shedding of the old. I had touched the
place inside me where something utterly unknowable was coming into being. How strange it felt to be so certain of something
that had no form or reflection. But I knew there would be, for
the inner would come into the outer, the old would give way to
the new, and a part of me would die, as indicated in the dream.

I wanted annihilation, the death of the ego and the dawning
awareness of the higher Self, and I assumed this was the death in
the dream. As afraid as I was, I wanted to be awake in the Self,
the state of consciousness Pearlie had been hinting at for months
now – a state where life is, and yet a separate self is not. A Sufi
teacher describes this state of union:

*In the experience of union all duality disappears. There
is neither wayfarer nor goal. This is the state of fanâ,
annihilation. The lover is lost in the Beloved. Only the moth
consumed in the flames of love knows the true nature of fire,
but who is left to know? At the very center of his own existence
the lover discovers the truth of non-existence. The manifest
returns to the unmanifest and the cycle is completed.*[19]

I was not sure how this annihilation could happen. A few days passed and I was edgy and eager. The weather seemed to mimic my mood, and soon an autumn storm arrived.

I had grown accustomed to letting Pearlie go outside on her own and allowing her to return when she wanted. Usually she wandered around for twenty minutes or so, and then pawed at the door to come back in. But this night of the storm, Pearlie went outside and she did not come back.

I had let her out at seven, and by seven thirty the weather had changed and I became confused. For some reason she had not returned. By eight the wind had become furious and the rain was coming down hard as stones. Pearlie had never been out in bad weather without me. She was one of those dogs who cowered at thunder or loud noises.

In the previous months, my love for Pearlie had given me access to a deep ground of stability and simplicity. I touched into this space of peace, even as confusion and fear drew me out into the night to look for her. I was worried. I was afraid she was lost and scared by this weather. I wanted to find her and bring her home.

I went out on foot, and then in the car. I did not see her. I drove down the streets, and into all the empty driveways, my headlights scanning across the yards like that old game of German flashlight we had played as children decades before.

My neighbor had mowed the field behind his cottage, and I drove into it as far as my car could go. It was new and expansive space, and I had the feeling Pearlie had maybe gotten lost there.

My headlights scanned the fields, and into view came three slight deer. They weren't afraid, but stood there, first looking, then not looking, at me. The rain in the headlights sparkled and surrounded them. They were glowing in fireworks of wet light. I watched them for a while. I doubted my own commitment to finding Pearlie as enraptured as I was by their nobility and glistening beauty.

Later I went out again in the car, to scan yards past the community boundaries. Along a street, now quiet at such a late hour, a fox found me. With such confidence in its nighttime ways it ran for a while beside my car, on the other side of the road. When I stopped, it stopped. In the dark, with no cars coming, we rested there. I rolled down the window and we stared at each other for a while.

Then I drove on.

I did not find Pearlie. I returned to the house, and then, when warmed enough, I went back out. She'd been gone almost seven hours. I had the feeling she was lost for good, for where would she have gone that she could still return from after all that time?

I stayed in a state of prayer, this place of being that she had shown me over this last year. I stayed there and let my love emanate into the pearl, and let my sadness stream out into the wind.

It felt a strange betrayal – that I did not feel desperate, overwhelmed by anxiety or loss, that I did not call out to her directly. It felt like an abandonment of the outer Pearlie to trust that if I spoke within the pearl my call would go where it was needed. Yet I knew this inner pearl contained us both, and if I remained in this new space in my heart where everything is included and perfect, despite all the possibilities and losses, that all would be as it should.

I went to sleep at 2:30, leaving the door open for Pearlie if she could, after all that time and distance, come back. I could not imagine this was going to happen.

But an hour later I awoke with a start. I rose to look for her through the window. I could see nothing out in the darkness. But suddenly I saw her, right at my feet, curled up in her bed.

I turned on the light and she was wet and dirty, with giant

spiky burrs caught in her paws and on her legs. I felt how hard it must have been for her to walk home with all that stinging and pricking.

But she was back. Wet, and distant, and still. As though she had never been gone, and as though some part of her had stayed lost with the wind and all those midnight smells. I lay down next to her for a while, so glad to have her there, to be with her. I would have missed her if she had not returned, I thought. I gently stroked her and picked the burs from her paws and her coat. I cried a bit, imagining life without her. She opened her tired eyes to watch me for a moment, but it was as though she was still out in the dark and her eyes could not really see me from there. So she shut them again and just let me pet her.

Was this how it is? One can stay still and open, within peace even as drama and loss are happening around you? Even to those you love? Even to yourself? Is this how everything is stripped and stripped further away, and at the same time the Real grows and glows stronger in its own space, the only haven, and only possible way to sustain that which comes and goes? How strange it is, this betrayal of the illusion by the Real, I thought, lying next to Pearlie, stroking her wet ears, kissing dry her heavy eyelids.

Calls from home

Not long after the night Pearlie was away for so many hours, a call came from my landlord in California. When was I returning, he wanted to know? He asked me forcefully, as though irritated by my absence. I soon learned why. Raccoons were coming in the cat door. It seemed that the man subletting the house was traveling a lot, and while he was gone another friend who was helping to care for the house found raccoons coming in and making a mess of the kitchen. With my sub-letter's absence, and no one sure when I would be returning, my landlord and my friend were feeling overwhelmed by the need to manage the raccoons.

"When are you returning?" he demanded.

I was shaken by this sudden input from my life back home, this cry for attention from my house and cat. I tried to put off answering. I had been gone four months but I didn't want to think of returning. I felt that something was trying to grow, and I felt it needed time. I told him I would talk to the sub-letter and also try to find other people to help with the house so he did not have to worry.

I called my sub-letter to find out his future travel schedule, for I felt if he could stay in the house he could take care of the cat-door issue. But I received another shock when he told me he was unexpectedly vacating my house in a month.

What was I to do? I asked friends in California to help with the cat door, but I received more shocks when they said they either could not or did not want to help. There seemed no solution to the difficulties back home.

I wasn't sure that I should return to California; I had been waiting for something in the outer world to pull me once and for all away from the dynamics of dependence that had marked my time near my teacher. But the only thing coming was the need for attention back home. Was I to follow this need? The practicality of it seemed assuring, and yet I was confused.

I was determined not return into that old dynamic. I called a volunteer agency in California and discovered a training course for volunteer work with children that would take place in a few months. The timing was perfect. I did not want to return to California without something in outer life to orient me away from my teacher. So I planned a return in January, which would give me another month away and would give my landlord a time-line he could depend on. I trusted that those five months would be what I needed.

As soon as I made the decision to return, I felt a rush of love. I realized I had kept my love for my teacher aside during those months in Connecticut, allowing a different love to nurture my life. But I was not worried. I had the feeling both loves could live together somehow, without one diminishing the other. The thought of seeing my teacher again flooded me with joy and the sense of possibility.

I could feel this new life coming. The energy of love and longing, hope and new beginnings, overwhelmed me. I had confidence that the peace and simplicity I had begun to feel would be the ground for a new way of living. I could be on my own and also begin the work with my teacher that he had promised would come.

I called my landlord to tell him my plans.

The next day, another call came. It was my friend Nan calling with a message from my teacher, who had heard of my plans to drive home.

I had been standing when the phone rang, and I sat down on the stool by the breakfast bar when I heard the tone of her voice. Her words were held tight in her throat, sounding both anxious and over-excited.

I was not to come back, she said. In front of our meditation group my teacher had slammed his fist on the floor and told Nan to tell me he did not want see or talk to me. He said that maybe in five or ten years I could return.

There were no further instructions.

Betrayal

For a long time I was consumed by fear and panic.

Was I panicked because I would not see my teacher – this person I loved so much – for years? Was it because I was stranded suddenly with no life, and no idea how to live? Was it because I had failed my teacher? Or because I had failed myself?

It was all these things and more. Everything felt lost. Hope, opportunity, love, my one chance to take an important spiritual step – all these things felt destroyed. In my panic I could not even touch upon my love for Pearlic. And I feared that it had been an illusion too, and so was destroyed as well.

I knew I had made a terrible mistake, but I did not know what it was. What had I done?

I had heard it said again and again by my teacher that on the path everything has to go so the human being only wants God. Perhaps the best way for this to happen is through betrayal. We hold on to thoughts or ideas that suit us, and sometimes we are even lied to, only to have life circumstances or the words or actions of the teacher destroy those concepts.

I had suffered the first betrayal years ago when the constant love and attention of my teacher had suddenly been withdrawn. A ground for relating to him and even for relating to myself was destroyed then. Now, deeper and more subtle hopes and expectations could not hold within this new picture of my life. I had believed my teacher. I had believed that I would only be gone from him for six months. I had believed that my life and work was with him. But these beliefs were destroyed now. The deception was like acid, dissolving deep and subtle threads of attachment, thought, and belief.

Almost worse than the sense of having been betrayed by my teacher was the feeling of having been betrayed by my own inner understanding. A confidence and trust in my inner experience was decimated. I had believed my dreams, which all pointed to an opening to life and love. I trusted that I would be given something in outer life to help me pass through these openings, as my teacher indicated before I left him, and I myself prayed so deeply for. But nothing new had come. The only outer need that demanded my attention – the need to attend to my house in California – was a strange trick and a way to fail.

Amidst my fear and confusion, all I could do was offer a prayer – the prayer of one of the great masters of our lineage, which asks for the power to remain forever under the shelter of the teacher. Not the shelter I had imagined, a shelter under which I was protected and loved. Rather I prayed to remain in the shelter of willingness and commitment. I did not want to lose this one thin thread – this thread of commitment between my teacher and me, this thread of service that existed far beyond outer nearness. If I could hold on to this thread of real belonging something within me would withstand this devastation.

And I tried to feel the potential of that moment. I understood that this betrayal could take me from one system of relating to life into another much more limitless experience of life. And I assume this is the point of betrayal on our path. Thoughts, ex-pectations, beliefs that define one's relationships can no longer hold. Structures of the psyche are disintegrated in a vortex of nothingness.

I understood that my role was to accept these new circum-stances. It was not easy, for I felt tremendous resistance – confu-sion, terror, and grief, all took their turns rearing their heads. But I tried to keep going, addressing the outer details of my life one by one, hoping my inner state would change in time.

In the old days it was my teacher who told me what to do. He made suggestions about how to live, what to focus on, what to write about. But now? All I had was me, and I was lost in this new world of aloneness and confusion, wondering how anything at all could grow in this desert scorched now, it seemed, by way too much sun.

A short time later my landlord told me that the house where I had been living would be put on the market to be sold, and that I had to return to pack it up and ship my belongings to Connecticut. I was terrified by the idea of being in that small town as an exile, ashamed to run into people who all knew I had been told to stay away, all knew I had made a grave mistake, that my teacher was done with me for years.

I did not have a place for my furniture, or my cat. I lived in a summer house – temporary and already fully furnished. What would I do with everything?

I needed something to ground me and distract me from my inner fears and panic. My aunt had a number of friends in the area, and I asked her to inquire about job possibilities. She called an artist with a jewelry store and they hired me part time. It was winter now, dark and snowy. But it was good to get out and do something. I would drive the twenty minutes to a neighbouring town and work three days a week in a pretty little jewelry and gift shop, filled with Christmas shoppers. The other workers were young – in their twenties – and I appreciated being around their distracting energy and enthusiasm. In the quiet moments I heard about their boyfriends or their career plans. Part of me felt grateful for the diversion, another part felt the absurdity of being forty-one years old and starting over in a jewelry store.

I found some volunteer work, too. There would be a training course for a volunteer job at a children's agency in a month. Till then, I did office work in a homeless shelter.

And Pearlie? I could not find my love for her. She too seemed more disoriented than ever, and one day she started coughing badly. It seemed to come from nowhere – a hacking cough from deep in her chest. I followed her as she paced anxiously around the house, trying to comfort her. But she was in her own discomfort and I could not help. I thought it meant the cancer had returned, the final sign that all hope for us was lost. I took her to the vet certain that he would tell me that her time was up, certain I had failed so completely that she was allowed to give up on me too, as my teacher had done.

This time, my relief was great when the x-rays did not show cancer. She was still healthy, at least according to the tests. The coughing persisted, on and off, and this worried me. The vet suggested allergy medicine, which worked somewhat. We both kept going. We kept to ourselves. Though I could not feel "ourselves" together at all.

Belonging

In time, my panic settled into a deep stream of shame and insecurity. I knew I had made a terrible mistake. I had betrayed my teacher, God, my Self, not the other way around. I should have known that returning to California meant I was not claiming my own life and light.

And more deeply, and perhaps more importantly, I understood that all those months of preparation so something new could come into my outer life had been undermined by a hidden inner dynamic of self-protection. I had not seen her in my dreams, but the dark spider must have still been alive inside me, devouring new life even before it could grow. That inner darkness – my own control and defense mechanisms – had been working to make sure I did not surrender into the aloneness and unpredictability of something truly new and alive.

I had failed, absolutely. Deep inside, I had not wanted real spiritual life. I had wanted the old memories, which protected me and kept me separate and safe.

What does it do to a human being when all her efforts are for nothing? When so much attention and care have come to naught?

My awareness of my own inadequacy and helplessness grew and grew over the weeks since the horrifying message from my teacher. All I could do was allow the genuine and deep feelings of failure and shame to pour into my consciousness.

These feelings of failure were frighteningly vast and seemed as old as time. It was as though not just this failure, but oceans and oceans of failure were flooding me with feelings of inadequacy. How would I ever serve God if I was capable of this kind of failure? How could I ever trust myself again? Trust anything again? I sank into a humility and vulnerability I had never known.

As days and weeks passed, the shame and fear receded leaving me in a state of pure weakness, as though I had survived a shipwreck and I lay barely alive on a foreign shore. I could not lift my head for the weakness.

But from that weakness something intimate and powerful revealed itself. Deep within my helplessness, I discovered a relationship of love and service I had never known. I felt myself humble in failure, and suddenly I was humble before That which I had failed. It was as though I finally met the source of power and love I had longed to serve.

This power first made itself known as I lay in bed one night after a long day at the jewelry store. Tired, and utterly sad, I prayed for help. Something came into my consciousness like a slow motion shooting star, a ball of light far away in the darkness. It was pale yelllow colored and spinning fast, revealing itself from a place of total emptiness. In that moment of feeling its presence, I bowed down and woke up.

In my failure, I met That which I had failed. In my weakness I met That which was all-powerful. In my humility, I met That which was great.

I had been searching and searching. But something else was much better at searching, and had found me first.

Was it God? Was it my teacher? Was it the power of our lineage? My Self? I didn't know. But I awoke within an awareness of absolute service. All that mattered to me was this inner reality of surrender, and the tender belonging it drowned me in. This relationship had been revealed. But could I live it for the rest of my life, while wanting nothing else? I did not know. I wanted another chance, and I hoped, one day, it would be given.

Spinning love into the world

Something within had woken up in service. The power and intimacy of that revelation lasted a few weeks and slowly disappeared leaving only an awareness that I had to keep going. I worked at the jewelry store and looked for jobs with willpower and a sense of duty. The days seemed cold and I barely felt anything at all except my own willingness to persevere.

A month after his first call, my landlord called to tell me that he was not selling my old house after all. He had found someone else to live there, someone happy to take care of my cat. This task of having to return and pack my belongings and bring back my cat was no longer a burden. He even offered to mail me anything I wanted to keep. I was so grateful. I felt it was such a gift, a well-needed reprieve from the horrendous details of my situation, for I still could not face returning to that town and all the loss it represented.

By necessity I considered a new life in Connecticut. But what, and how? I was over forty, and had been living in retreat for the last ten years, told by my teacher that I would only do spiritual work. Where would I find a normal job? How could I make a living? I had no idea where to begin.

Late that winter, I was given a clue. I woke up one morning into the feeling-less dissociation that marked my days. But instead of just getting out of bed and starting the day in this state, as I had done many times before, I felt something inside me that seemed new. Deep in the pit of my stomach, something was alive and making itself known. It was an energy or substance. It had the slight warmth of love.

It was Pearlie.

The energy of Pearlie was alive inside me, and it drew my consciousness towards it. Then, guided by my attention, it streamed outward into the room.

Lying in bed, amazed, I remembered the dream I'd had so many weeks ago of the six dancing Alisons. In that dream, Alison had thrown herself out of the depth of her being five times until there were six of her, belly dancing together in a beautiful flowing pattern. I saw now how I had misunderstood that dream. I had assumed the dream meant that I was doing this dance already.

But this morning as I went into my belly consciously and drew up this life and love (this living love!) and projected it outwardly, I realized that the dream had actually been showing me *how* to do this! Alison was showing me how to *begin* this dance. She was teaching me what to do, pointing to my own being as a source of love and power that could be projected outward so a dance could begin. All those months I could have been practicing.

How wrong I had been about so much. Nothing was going to step up and draw me into life, as I had hoped. Either I had killed that new life with my hidden dynamics, or it was simply never going to happen that way.

It dawned on me how responsible I was in the creative process of life. For as I breathed this inner substance outward, everything seemed to include a subtle dimension previously absent, as though an inner love could enliven manifestation. The room felt filled with energy, each piece of furniture seemed to have its own charms, everything appeared to me shimmering awake. If I did this practice at night, my house felt a sacred place – watchful –holding me in care as I let myself rest.

Of course life is alive just as it is. And of course life is complete just as it is. Yet how much more alive everything seemed when I breathed love outward, or when I touched a table while recognizing its beauty, or when I drank a glass of water with gratitude. I could not deny the power of this practice. I had loved Pearlie and watched her come alive. Now if I loved other things with the same attention, they, too, transformed.

My teacher had told me that human consciousness played a role in recognizing the divine perfection of creation. Now I was glimpsing a different aspect of that responsibility. I was being shown a way to participate, not just witness, the sacredness of the manifest. It seemed to be a hidden purpose of human consciousness I might never understand.

It wasn't fun or easy to do this practice. But I did it by necessity. Without it, my life felt so empty. But after projecting this inner substance outward, there was a feeling of communion. I felt strongly that consciously enacting this dream would begin to connect me to life again, could repair some damage that had been done during my recent shock.

The morning when this spinning began was a strange morning. I saw how alone I was, and also how powerful human beings are. Pearlie had taken me to a place inside myself that could nourish so much in the outer world. The energy of the Pearl was to be shared.

Something else became clear. I had worried about finding a job. I worried about finding the right job for me. I had a few interviews, which had not worked out, and those failures left me anxious and searching. But now I felt certain it did not matter what kind of work I did. I just needed to begin. I needed to find something – anything – to do.

I was the spider, I just needed to go out and spin.

I continued looking for work – all over the country. I started my volunteer job with neglected children, which was almost as dull as I had dreaded, but I did not care. I tried to project love into every day, as much as I could remember. The days were joyless and plodding, because while the love could flow from me and even come back to me with its warmth, it had nothing to do with me. This was a strange paradox that left me both confused and a bit lonely. But I tried not to dwell on my feelings, and focused, instead, on what was in front of me.

5

New life

And according to what was
traced on my heart
were the words of my letter.
I remembered that I was a
son of royal parents,
and my noble birth asserted itself.
I remembered the pearl,
for which I had been sent to Egypt...

Hymn of the Pearl

An open door

I am with my teacher and some others from our group. We are talking about a destructive energy that kills things just as they are about to come into manifestation. Inwardly, I recognize the energy of the spider from other dreams. Someone says, "Hilary used to have so much of this energy, but now it is gone."

My teacher nods his head slowly and looks away. He says, so softly:

"At some point there is just an open door."

Changes in Pearlie

Sometimes grace is the only explanation for change. The previous months both in California and Connecticut, I had become aware of the destructive energy inside me. I had tried to nurture Pearlie and the life she opened me to, but had I really done anything to transform the Hag and her eight-legged friend?

To be told in my dream that suddenly this energy was gone, and to consider that an inner doorway was now always open, filled me with awe and gratitude. Perhaps finally my heart was open to the Creator and creation both, allowing the energies of the beyond to flow effortlessly where they are needed – even all the way into this world.

I knew that the dream heralded deep changes. But outwardly I was facing roadblocks. The resumes I'd sent out had come to nothing. It was not easy finding a job being away from the work-force for so long. I was frustrated by not getting more responses from my resumes, but I could understand how I must have looked as a candidate for these jobs, most of which could more appropriately be filled by an eager, intelligent, recent college graduate with conviction and drive. I was over forty, with no recent job experience, and no clear interest other than mysticism. Who in their right mind would hire me?

But I wasn't disheartened. For while I knew the next step was to create an outer life of some kind, I sensed that the deeper meaning of the dream was about love, and how love and light from the inner worlds can now flow into life regardless of where I was or what I was doing.

Besides, spring's sudden presence after my first New England winter in twenty years cheered me up. All around me the world was proving the persistence of life.

How much I loved Pearlie those spring days! Since the shock of being told not to return to my home and my teacher, this love had filtered slowly back through the panic and emptiness. My inner Pearl – vast and glowing with endless light – seemed to have a special place for the outer Pearlie, and every moment that sweet creature looked at me or I looked at her, this inner light flamed upwards in love.

Pearlie had come to mean so much to me, and I was deeply disturbed when I noticed how strangely she was acting. Those late winter months, her independence slowly changed into withdrawal. She did not seem to want my affection, or my comfort. After our morning walk, she retired to the bedroom and never used her bed in the living room, where I did my writing. In earlier days, she would lie in the living room bed to be near me. Then I could pet her more often, and she would watch me and sometimes approach me if she wanted my attention. But now she stopped that completely, and this bed was never used.

When I took a break and went into the bedroom to pet her, she rarely moved to reveal her belly. She never seemed to invite me in like she used to. In fact, it seemed like she had forgotten me. She would walk around the house to get water or to go outside and she just ignored me. Sometimes I managed to catch her walking from the bedroom to her water bowl and I would force her to let me rub her belly and chest while she stood trapped between my legs. I could see that she was grateful, as though she had forgotten I could make her feel better, but then she would move away, as though agitated and eager to be alone.

Most dogs come to their owners for love, but Pearlie had always been different. Now it was as though I had to go to extremes to remind her of my existence. When she felt me near she enjoyed the attention, but I could feel her surprise, and in that moment of surprise I could feel how forgotten I had been.

Outside, when we went for walks, she still had her moments of excitement, running at me for a moment and teasing me to chase her. But in general she became slower. The winter grass held no interest for her, and she no longer rolled in it. I think it would have been hard on her hips and legs, which were now stiffer than ever.

Occasionally she would jump in the air, or run at me with her big eyes wide open, and I would feel a surge of happiness. These were moments of instant joy and connection, which became more and more valuable the more rare they were.

But one morning what had begun as a slight cough a month before had grown into coughing episodes during which she had trouble breathing and swallowing. Each episode lasted about ten minutes during which she paced around the house, coughed, tried to drink water, or tried to get outside to eat grass so she could throw up.

At first she just had one or two episodes a day, and the vet thought she had a mild cold or allergy. But on one particular day after she had thrown up twice, I knew something was very wrong and I took her back to the clinic.

Our vet was a young man who always spoke to Pearlie in a way that a woman might, with love and with care. I liked and trusted him with Pearlie. He didn't notice anything wrong when he examined her, but he took some blood, which later revealed a very low thyroid level.

He suggested a deeper problem might be causing the thyroid issue. I didn't really understand what he meant, and perhaps I just did not want to think she was suffering from something more serious or less treatable. So we put her on thyroid medicine, which helped the coughing only slightly and did nothing for her increasing malaise.

The coughing episodes were hard on me. When Pearlie began to cough, she became anxious and paced around the house desperately. Though I tried to be with her, to follow her, or encourage her to relax during these episodes, I really could not help her. I would try to catch her as she was pacing, and hold her between my legs so I could stroke her. Sometimes she let me do this, but mostly she just pushed on past.

I just wanted Pearlie to rest and to be happy. But her sickness in addition to her general withdrawal, concerned me. I became afraid that she would have a coughing episode when I left her, so I did not leave the house for more than an hour or two at a time. My jewelry store job had ended, as the owner did not need my help after the Christmas rush. And now I was glad none of my resumes resulted in job offers, because Pearlie needed my attention.

I wanted to be there for Pearlie, but one morning in March, Pearlie showed me why she had been there with me.

The meaning of life

Since the day my teacher had instructed me to attend to Pearlie, I had found all sorts of ways to love her. I would find love inside myself and then direct it into her with my eyes. Or, I would sit next to her and use every breath to wrap her in a gentle cloud of love. This could bring me into a very soft and simple place in which I felt Pearlie and I were together.

Or I would turn my attention inside myself to where I already felt connected to her, where I loved some kind of inner Pearlie, where we already seemed together. And from there I would just sit with her and touch her, hoping that she could absorb through my presence this love I felt inside.

Sometimes I would look at her long eyelashes, or her cool, spongy nose, or the long hairs of her ears which twitched with every heart beat, and I caught how I smiled to myself, how I felt a protective joy at these parts of her, and how I let that joy flow back to her like a reflection of her own glory.

I had come to love loving Pearlie. I loved finding where I recognized her beauty, where I felt us together, where I appreciated her whole being. Then I would try to give it all back to her. It had not always been like this. I had not always liked taking the time or making the effort to love her. Sometimes that task had seemed like an impenetrable roadblock, or worse – a diversion from what I loved most.

I had resented Pearlie so much those first months when my teacher told me to spend time with her, not him. I had only wanted the love that I had for him – a love that was exciting and dynamic, a love that came with no effort but flowed continuously. Focusing on Pearlie seemed a Herculean task designed to turn me away from this other love, but which had never really borne fruit.

Almost always I had to make an effort, take a leap of some kind, find an inner space that was not always so accessible, and then love her from there. Like my practice of spinning – even with Pearlie I had to make this effort to bring love outward from some deep inside space. I was willing to make this effort because my teacher told me to learn from her.

But that March morning I was shocked to discover that the effort was no longer needed. Love was present as it had never been.

Pearlie had been agitated all that morning. After breakfast and our walk she did not want to lie down again in the bedroom. She paced around the kitchen but didn't want to go outside. I supposed her unwillingness to lie down had to do with being uncomfortable, with her stiffness, with not wanting to feel the discomfort of resting back down on legs that had just woken up and stretched out. So I held her while she was standing and massaged her. She looked at me with need, and her wide open eyes made me sad and uncertain.

So I encouraged her to go for another walk. It was so sunny outside, so warm and full of spring. The ground had that damp warmth to it, as though there had been a warm rain, but I guess it was just dew and sun mixing themselves together in a springtime cocktail.

She seemed happy outside in the morning air, and I was glad I had encouraged her. When we returned to the house, she immediately went to lie down in her bed. At first I sat down at the table to write, but I realized I just wanted to be with her. I followed her into the bedroom, into the cool space where the morning light only slightly entered. I found an old blanket and put it next to her bed and sat down with her. She did not adjust herself so I could pet her stomach; she just lay there seemingly unaware of me, not caring that I was petting her.

But I wanted to stay with her. I smoothed out the scraggly hair on her cheeks, I stroked her sides, and tried to massage her legs. She just lay there – still and near sleep. As my hands found their way around and through her soft fur I felt something I had never felt before. I felt my love for her happening naturally, without effort, without conscious attention. I felt the love come through my hands and I felt that love flow into her body.

It was a strange and impersonal feeling. She wasn't looking at me; there was no outer sign of recognition, no emotion, no intention or effort. Love was just coming from me and she was receiving it. I felt her drink it in. It was like her body was a magnet pulling me into her. It was just happening.

I sat there in the dark for almost an hour. She seemed to drift in and out of sleep. I cried sometimes, and then just pet her in the softness I felt around us. There wasn't even really a Pearlie or a me, yet we were both so present. Life, love, and awareness were all present.

That day and the following days, loving Pearlie was simple and full. I could feel her through the tips of my fingers, through the pressing of my palm, through my whispering kisses. I could feel her feel me, I could feel her pull my love further in.

That favorite spot of mine, the soft, soft fuzz at the base of her ear where her ear joined her cheek – how I loved touching that spot.

Nothing mattered to me but this exchange of love. It's the strangest thing to discover. I think you first have to do it – you have to try to love something or someone for years and forever, as though it will never amount to anything, as though it isn't really true or real. You have to do it out of a deeper love or hidden obligation, with no expectation of success, without even *knowing* what you are doing.

And then when this new way dawns, when it approaches softly and completely, then there is such awe and glory and magic.

Something was here. Something of me, or Pearlie, or this love I knew from the inner, had finally come *here*. It had been focused away for so long, far away, onto my teacher or into the emptiness beyond form. And everything in me had resisted letting go of those heights. But now I could feel that love was part of the physical world, flowing with an intelligence of its own.

I loved Pearlie that morning, and all the next mornings, in a way I cannot describe because it is so simple and so wondrous at the same time. What else matters in this world? What else could have any purpose besides this giving and receiving of love?

I had found a depth of meaning within my life I could never have fathomed without her. My beautiful Pearlie, my soft angel, the one who brought me here. Pearlie did it. She brought *me* here.

And then she left me here alone.

The Black River

A few miles from my house, a river winds itself through a wide and gentle marshland in graceful swirls and spirals and then enters into the sea. It is my favorite part of town, and I ran by it when I wanted to run for a long time.

It is called the Black River, and its water is dark and slow moving. On a sunny day it sparkles with light. In the winter, it is surrounded by grasses and reeds of infinite shades of sand and straw, bowed down to the ground by the wind and snow. It is the home of gulls and egrets, cormorants and other birds.

Sometimes when I ran by the Black River, I could feel inside myself the river's fullness and how it swelled over the sand and soft grass when it rose at the high tide. And I also felt inside me the presence of those marsh pools it had formed as some marshes do – circular pools of water, and in this case black water like strange and glassy tunnels into the ground.

Soon after that morning when Pearlie showed me the hidden meaning in my life, she died. A few nights later, I was told in a dream that Pearlie's death had taken me to the Black River.

Was it the grief that had dissolved me into this flowing darkness, these glistening black waters? Was it the anguish of having lost her, having to live without her?

After she died I was lost, again. But this was not a dissociated lost; it was an absorption in something beautiful and deep. Was I feeling grief or longing? Was it loss or love? Was this deep rhythmic flow the movement of life or death? After days and days of crying I lost track entirely. Love and loss and sadness and murmurs of belonging all merged together and I floated and drowned in it all.

Was this the blackness I had dreamed about for years – the blackness of the seal of communion? The blackness of the spider's abdomen?

I felt like a corpse on a river – slowly dissolving into nothing but the thick eternal flow. This was where I belonged, absorbed in this river, in its black emptiness, in its swirling love and sunken treasures of golden longing.

Crucifixion

Losing Pearlie was a final sorrow and a final letting go. And yet it was not just the loss of my dear friend that tore open my heart, and opened me to the deeper background of flowing darkness. It was the part I played in her death, deciding to put her to sleep. It was the utter unfairness and difficulty of being all alone with no idea what to do or how to do it. She was nearing the end of her time with me, that much I knew. But I brought her to her death, and that terrible responsibility was devastating.

I would say that her death was sudden, except somewhere I knew it was coming. A few weeks before her death, I dreamt that Pearlie and I were on a dangerous cliff. She led me down a steep path to a black body of water below. I followed her into the water, longing to swim naked in this beauty. When I returned to the shore, Pearlie had disappeared, and I was alone with a love I had never experienced before. When I awoke, I knew the path had worked. The suffering, the losses, they had all led me to a love that was eternal.

The dream showed me that Pearlie's work with me was over. She had brought me down from a precipice into a darkness that is part of life, and then left me in love. A few days later, she had shown my waking consciousness that a new love was present.

Those last weeks Pearlie had seemed so withdrawn and besieged by the strange coughing. I should have – I could have – seen that she was leaving me.

Her leaving began one night toward the end of March. She was not able to rest in her bed after our brief evening walk. I tried to comfort her but she wandered anxiously from one room to another, standing at the door to go out, back to the water bowl, around and around the house.

I lay down in bed myself, hoping that my resting would encourage hers. It didn't, and from my bed I heard her continue the unsettled pacing. I rose to be with her, and I followed her around for a while, trying to steady her, trying to hold her and love her, but I was so confused and afraid. As she neared the southern wall of my bedroom she began to shake, and she fell down and closed her eyes.

I expected her to die right then. But Pearlie didn't; instead she stayed unconscious for a while and then very, very slowly opened her eyes to orient herself back to this world. I held her; I stroked her. When she was conscious enough for me to leave her side, almost an hour later, I went into the living room to call my vet. It was too late to reach him, and I was referred to an emergency clinic in a town an hour away. The receptionist there reassured me, saying that sometimes a dog can have a seizure and recover very quickly. So I went back to the bedroom, hopeful that Pearlie would be all right.

But she didn't seem all right. She could not rest, and the seizure had made her blind. After two hours of lying down against the wall, she began to awkwardly pace the room, stumbling as though drunk, not seeing the furniture. She kept bumping into the beds and bureau, and I could not stop her. I had to shut the bedroom door and move the furniture around so she could not hurt herself.

Every now and then I could force her to lie down for a moment, but she did not stay in bed. When I was certain she would not sleep, but could not hurt herself, I lay down and slept an hour or two. It was a thin sleep and eventually I just woke to be with her.

I called our vet as soon as he was in the office the next morning. He was somber, and told me to bring Pearlie in to the office right away. He explained that there had been a power outage

– a truck had run into a power line down the road – and all the electricity was out and the roads were blocked. He said he would alert the police to my arrival. When I crossed the barricade and pulled into the parking lot two firemen approached, and one of them carried Pearlie's slack body into the building.

In the cool office, dark without lights, the vet examined Pearlie. She was still blind, still stumbling around. He was certain this seizure was related to the underlying cause of her other disturbances, the cause of the thyroid problem and the recent increase in disorientation. Slowly I understood what he was telling me. His opinion was that Pearlie was dying – if not in the next five minutes, certainly in the next day or two. He assumed Pearlie had a brain tumor that could not be detected in blood work, and without cat scans, an MRI, and immediate surgery Pearlie would suffer more seizures and die.

It can be so strange hearing news like that. I don't think I really heard it. Somehow I had been living with Pearlie in a sacred and protected space, and I had not let in the outer world and its violent ways.

You see, Pearlie had not been my dog, she had been a mystery. She had not been vulnerable to anything of this world – to the cancer that had almost killed her two years before, to the drivers on the nighttime roads that could so easily have missed seeing her odd and slow meanderings, to the night that had claimed her for all those hours a few months ago. The Pearlie I knew was not subject to the laws of this world.

Maybe with her, I wasn't either. And maybe this needed to change.

That day and that evening I prayed constantly. I felt as though I found the energy of my teacher and my tradition and it seemed alive and present with us. I felt all my love come through my hands to her body, when she let me touch her.

I remembered vividly some of what I had read about crones and hags, the old women who lived as part of nature, who understood life and death and how to navigate between the worlds. I tried to summon them; I asked them all to come and help Pearlie leave this place, help her make it to the next world. They seemed to circle around us in a clearing at the edge of the woods near a river, waiting to carry Pearlie on.

That second night she was as agitated as before, and we were awake together except for a few brief moments of rest.

A call in the morning from the vet was another shock, another rupture in the barriers between the outer world and the protected space of Pearlie and me. He assured me this would continue, that Pearlie would not recover, and he encouraged me as he had done the day before to consider an end to her suffering.

I think I made a strange choice that morning. I felt myself allow the restrictions of this world to enter ours. I let myself allow Pearlie to be part of the comings and goings of life. I let myself understand that she was ill, and dying.

If I had not been so confident that her work with me was complete, I would not have allowed myself to consider putting her down. But she had done so much for me, and now she was leaving. She seemed so distant. Pacing, she seemed to be walking an endless road, away and further away.

I decided to bring her to the vet that afternoon and have her put to sleep.

I felt that if I chose to love and nurture her she would stay with me. Despite her outer indifference, Pearlie loved me so much, and she knew how much I loved her. I thought that I could, if I wanted to, keep us protected in this magical space a bit longer. I felt my love for her was so strong, and her willingness to do what I needed so complete, that she would come back for a while if I asked her to.

I also sensed that her return would never be complete. She might come back, but a part of her would be gone, and the rest would be more uncomfortable than before. And I did not want this for her.

That final morning with Pearlie, I pulled her bed into the sunlight that was streaming in the living room through the sliding glass doors with the view of the Sound. I carried her there, and for a long time we lay there together in the sun. We were warm. We were together and resting. I just stroked her and loved her.

Later, I guided her outside, carrying her down the little steps to the grass. She lay there for a while, a bit more awake in the fresh air. But when we went back inside, she fell heavily on the tile floor of the kitchen, and lay there, collapsed.

I put a small pillow under her head, and left her while I drove the ten minutes to the vet and picked up some tranquilizers so that she would be very calm when the vet gave her the shot to end her life. And when the tranquilizers were working, I lifted her into the back of my car and drove her to the vet's office.

In a moment she was gone. I watched as suddenly she went from being with me to being entirely absent. I thought she must have been here only by the slightest thread – the slightest breath of love, for she was gone as though she never existed. There was no discernable moment of transition. One instant to the next, from something I loved so completely to nothing at all.

I couldn't help but fear I had done the wrong thing in having her put down. I prayed to know if it had been the right or wrong decision. The only dream I had the next few nights was the dream in which I was shown the stark and infinitely winding Black River, and was told that Pearlie's death had taken me there.

I felt that this was true. Her death and my role in it had broken me apart and opened me to new depths. I could feel this river of blackness, gentle, wide and endless, flowing way beyond issues of right or wrong, questions of being together or alone. Some part of me was flowing in this new space so full and so empty, which seemed to rise up with the tide, and empty out with the tide. What moon was determining that rising and emptying was unknowable to me.

Over the coming weeks, I could feel something reaching back to me through this fullness, reminding me of quicker movements and different shades of light and color. It was like the tender stirrings of wings on river birds brushing against my cheeks on their way to and from their nests and the small ones waiting there to be fed. With the Black River, this was all that was on offer… those gentle birds, their quickly moving feathers, stroking, fluttering, here and there, nothing to hang on to, only a vibration or slight hum resonating from within that magic blackness.

I was sad for a long time about Pearlie. I did the things I had been doing before she died, but now I was in a sort of haze. I kept writing, I worked with my volunteer client, and kept looking for full-time work.

I noticed that I did not turn to memories of my old life quite as much as I had before. Those too were fading. I was not as compelled to use my separation from my teacher as a place to project my sadness. But losing one's projections is not easy, even if they are painful projections. I felt strangely more lost than ever.

A week after Pearlie died I was taking a long run. I ran across the causeway, past all the swans, up toward town, and down a small back street. I was near the crossroads that took me left between the Black River and Long Island Sound. The sun was in and out of the clouds. It was springtime for certain, and when the sun came through all the colors were vivid and bright.

I was crying a bit. I turned a little corner into the sun. There, coming toward me on the left, I could see a group of people. The sun was in my eyes, and so were the tears, and I was not really sure what I was looking at until I approached them and noticed the long and heavy wooden cross bearing down on one man's shoulders. There was even a thorny crown at the top of the cross.

I had forgotten that it was nearly Easter. This was Good Friday, and they were re-enacting the crucifixion.

What a strange sight – this man carrying a large and heavy wooden cross aided by a few companions, surrounded by a group of people, walking down this small Connecticut street.

Jesus and the disciples in LL Bean. I didn't know whether to laugh or just cry harder.

I passed them, my eyes down, not wanting them to see my face, wet with tears.

It was the crucifixion. And I understood deep inside something about this terrible experience of being with God in this temporal and transient life. How God might have to split things apart, again and again, in order for those who love Him to awaken more and more deeply in the eternal.

A new harmony

In the weeks and months after Pearlie's death, I kept myself consciously involved on this deep level of spinning love into the world. With Pearlie gone I had no reason to go outside as I used to. It had been on those walks with her, slowly moving through gentleness of the neighborhood, that I had begun the daily practice of seeing all life as it was – sparkling and alive, a reflection of oneness and even in odd moments, joy.

So now it was just me alone first thing in the morning. Still cold, I would open the giant sliding glass door and sit on the threshold with a scarf around my neck, enjoying the contrast of hot coffee with the cool morning air. Sitting on those weathered Adirondack chairs under the wisteria vines – still snaky and gray – looking toward the water, I could always feel this magic. I could always see and feel the divinity of the morning. All the birds sang it. All the grass reflected it upwards, outwards. The sea moved with it. Life was full of God's love; life was in a state of praise and prayer. This was the most obvious and clear state of things.

It was still a conscious choice, a bit of effort, but not difficult in those first moments of the day, and I longed for the time that the effort was not needed, when I would be dancing with what I had brought alive, just like Alison danced with all those other Alisons. I wanted to be one of many, in a flow of dancing, playing my part but no longer solely responsible for maintaining the dance, no longer alone with all the instruments, setting out all the dance steps.

If it was true that Pearlie had taken me to the Black River, and that I was now – as I felt so strongly deep inside – part of this flow of dark water, lost in this heavy and subtle movement, then this connection should start to be reflected outside in a less effortful relationship with life. I longed for this, yet I knew from the past that inner changes happen much more quickly than outer changes. But I kept my eyes open, looking for hints at what was next. And when my cousin in New York suggested I move there, I found a spark of engagement light up within. I could find a job in the city, I felt certain.

My mother liked the idea of my move, and she offered to help me afford an apartment. I called a friend in the city who referred me to her friend who ran a textile business. He needed some marketing help, so I had found a part time job within a week of having the idea to move.

I began to sense a synchronicity and flow that I had last felt in the early years with my teacher, when things seemed to be given freely and with love. I was finding myself in the right place at the right time. Another's hand was busy, and I could see the handiwork.

Or should I say another's legs were busy spinning her own webs to help me spin mine. One night I dreamt:

I am in a new space, a new house. It has high ceilings, and at the top of the roof there is a skylight. I look way up and through the windows to the sky, which is blue and light.

Something catches my eye. I see – through the windows – a large, perfectly symmetrical spider web just above the roof. And then I see very clearly that there are a number of spider eggs in the web. But they are not naturally there – they are not being born. Rather, it is as though the eggs have been caught in the web. They too, are symmetrically placed.

I have in mind a "dream-catcher" from Native American mythology. I sense that the web has caught these eggs to protect me. I understand that the web catches and nullifies possible

*destructive energy that rises from me. I am very relaxed,
knowing that I am helped in this way.*

*And then I see her. I see her humongous body – huge brown
and black and furry. There is a giant spider on the roof. She is
maybe 500 pounds at least. I see so clearly her giant incisors
and her black eyes. She rests above the skylight by her web.*

*Despite her huge and grotesque body, I am not afraid. I am
deeply relaxed. And I awake with the feeling that she and her
web protect me.*

There had been a revolution. The spider, who had for so many
years worked below in my shadowy unconscious, was now above
in the light. The feminine force of creation was fully visible in the
ruling position, guiding what happens below her, her web not used
to trap me, but to trap and freeze seeds of my own negativity. For
that incredibly destructive power was now holding fast those small
egg sacks, which I imagined to be my own bursts of destructiveness.
But caught like that, they would never amount to much.

This force was now in its rightful place. The dark goddess, the
spinner, those old crones – rulers of life death and rebirth – were
now doing their work to help me live my life. All those months
ago, reading about crones and goddesses had only confused me.
Now something was becoming clear. There was a discernable
density in my life, a willingness to be more here, more grounded,
more part of the flow of life. (For who would think to rise up off
the earth, when that giant creature watched and waited above?)
And now things *were* flowing; things were happening around me.
I could see those crones' handiwork and how they kept life alive
and full of power and potential.

Most surprising, the feeling in the dream was one of deep
relaxation. Something inside me was calm, as though held by

resting forces. I felt it when I awoke, and it continued on, unabated. This relaxation seemed related to the Black River whose dark pull always kept me floating in heavy calm. The darkness was above, and the darkness was below. In between I was just where I needed to be.

There was so much to be grateful for. So much had been given to me. This dark energy, turned against me for so long, was released from my shadow, and now lived in the light of consciousness. Perhaps this giant spider energy was part of the spinning of love that I practiced daily. Perhaps I was helping her do her work of creating and protecting life in this world.

The weaving Goddess had her new place in my life, affecting my quality of life and my inner state. Things were happening quickly, and I was so relaxed. I was eager to move into the city and I took a train in to look for an apartment. It did not take long for me to find what I needed. It was a small studio apartment downtown, a five-floor walk up. As my realtor and I climbed the stairs there was more and more light. I noticed skylights in the ceiling, light was flooding the stairwell. It was not large; it was a studio after all. But I loved it. We entered a small kitchen/dining area, which also had a skylight above allowing light to brighten the whole apartment. At the edge of the tiny kitchen area were two French doors leading into the main room, which had a working fireplace, two windows and a few good closets. It was small, and so quiet. It looked out over an empty back alley where no cars could fit.

I was happy to be there. I went back to the realtor's office, which was in the next building, and signed all the paperwork. I wrote checks for three months rent and I moved in a week later.

This new harmony was wonderful, but it had a sense of humor. For on the fourth day of my new job I was fired.

I had finally moved through what was at times impenetrable resistance to become part of the world. Despite endless pain and frustration, incredible fear and loneliness, I finally surrendered into the ordinariness of being a normal working human being. Just to be fired and have to start all over again.

I certainly wouldn't have laughed if I had paid for my apartment myself. If I had been stuck with that rent and no job to pay for it. But my mother, so pleased that I had found something I wanted to do, was my financial security for the moment. Someone was having fun with my mother, too, and I hoped she was laughing! My mother has a good sense of humor, so I imagined she was.

I didn't really know why I was fired. The man who hired me called me on my cell phone as I was walking out of the subway after work and told me he had made a mistake hiring me. He could hardly explain himself. And certainly he had no capacity to tell me to my face. I was shocked, but had to laugh. I was in New York, and he had helped get me there. Somehow I was just grateful.

By now I knew that the most meaningful things in my life came with a sense of humor. I was amazed that I had taken this step, this momentous step into life, only to find myself with absolutely nothing to show for it. The joke was on me, that's for sure, and I laughed at myself all day and for days after.

6

Pearlie in the Big Apple

Life is a bitter ocean,
Yet drink it dry to find the Pearl of Heaven!
Don't worry about time and space.
Smash the moon! It still comes back!

Hsu Yun

Pearlie in the Big Apple

My relationship with Pearlie had been grounding in many ways. Without her, I was disoriented. My senses, my emotions, and my love, had been focused onto her. When she died, I was like a planet suddenly without its orbit.

Even my body was readjusting. Stepping out of bed the day after she died I noticed most of my hip and back pain vanished. Since our drive back to Connecticut, I had felt a great deal of pain deep in my legs and through my hips. I had visited a chiropractor as well as a massage therapist a number of times since the trip, but nothing had helped. Suddenly I was free of most of that discomfort. I assumed I had been trying to take on some of Pearlie's own hip and back pain, which had worsened in her later years. She had helped me so much; I must have been trying to help her.

Not all the changes felt good. My attention released from Pearlie and our simple space, I felt much more vulnerable to the outer and inner worlds. I felt out of control, overwhelmed by choices and events. And when I was fired after only four days of work, I realized that slipping back into normal life after so many years focusing on the inner would not be so straightforward.

But I was glad to notice that Pearlie wasn't really gone. She was everywhere in New York and I took refuge in those moments of feeling her presence. I had gone to Ikea to buy some furniture and came back to realize that most everything I'd chosen was either white or white and soft. I had a new white dining table, a large white plastic fruit bowl, a new white fuzzy wool rug, and two sheepskins – white and soft, just like Pearlie. Soon after I moved in, I realized the rug was made in such a way that the threads of wool shed endlessly. I had thought I would not have to worry about white fur on my clothes anymore with Pearlie gone, but I was mistaken. Still, I had to vacuum up those little balls of white fuzz; still, I had to keep my black clothes safe and separate.

My neighbor had a little herb garden on the fire escape we shared, and I saw Pearlie in the doves that came to the window every day. Two soft black-eyed little creatures came to eat seeds and rest on the metal grating. They weren't white, but their big eyes, soft brown chests and mournful sounds reminded me so much of Pearlie.

I wondered if someone hadn't made a key error. Months before on the tennis courts I had prayed to see God in everything. But here in New York, everywhere I looked I saw Pearlie.

Living with Pearlie meant living by new rules. My attention to Pearlie had brought me into a new space, and the laws of this space were different. As though different levels of reality had different laws, and being given even a bit of access to a new level required a new orientation, a new way to think and behave.

I was still deeply relaxed, as had been my state since the dream of the spider above my skylight. I could not really worry so much, and I felt strongly I did not have to do anything more – at least right then. And I felt so much help was being given to carry me through life.

Sometimes I tried to revert to how I used to live. I tried to worry about things. One morning after being fired I was walking down the street to a café. I was starting to feel a bit concerned, as the café I had my sights set on was an organic bakery, more expensive than other bakeries. I was mulling over the issue of money, trying actually to worry, to bring forth feelings of guilt or deep concern over going to an expensive café while unemployed. But the energy of despair was unavailable to me. I kept walking down the street, and out of the corner of my eye I noticed a piece of paper blowing in the wind, toward me. As it came closer,

I realized it was a bill. A breeze brought it right in front of my path and I stepped on it, reached down, and picked up ten dollars. I looked to my right, and a tall bald man in a shop window gave me a big smile and a thumbs up.

"New York is so friendly!" I thought, as I smiled back. I entered the bakery with plenty of money for the breakfast I had wanted. And that was the last time I worried about money.

Love was the currency in the new space. Love was everywhere, in many forms. The pigeons and the doves that flew outside my window were as majestic as the eagles that had flown around my cabin in Alaska. I could sit on my bed and watch them drop from the nearby rooftops, wings wide and tails fanned out, talons stretched forward to an invisible landing, streaking through the air with primordial power.

And the three old Chinese women who practiced tai chi in the nearby park worked with love in a hidden needlework, their open palms threading back and forth through invisible fabric, patching together the tears in the neighborhood. Whenever I ran by I felt them do their work, and it felt so deep and certain that I wanted to lie down in front of them on the grass and let them thread that energy through me too.

The rules of this new space required that I work with love. This meant maintaining presence and awareness, and respect for the unknown. Only if these conditions were met could I feel love coming from me into different situations, or work to spin it where it was absent. It wasn't easy living in this new world, which worked so differently from the old. I had to be reminded again and again about how things really were; I had to remember to see things the way Pearlie had.

And I made mistake after mistake. One day, a friend gave me tickets to a benefit dinner party honoring my boss from my first job, many years before, at an environmental organization in

Washington, DC. I was so happy to think of seeing my old boss again after almost fifteen years.

The meeting had that magic sparkle I knew so well, the sparkle that said, "be awake!" So many years and I would see him again! I had enjoyed working with him very much, and we had grown close. But in the years since, we had lost touch. I could not help but wonder why we were meeting now. I thought perhaps he would offer me a job to help me come more into the world.

But when I met him, and while we were laughing together like old friends never apart, he told me he was going to Asia for three years. There would be no job, no help in life, nothing for me.

I had already forgotten what Pearlie had shown me so many times, that love and beauty and other divine things don't necessarily have a point. They just are. There was no outer result from this meeting. I was just with my friend again, after so many years. Maybe our hearts had a secret conversation in a language I had yet to learn, and that was it.

How easily I had slipped into old ways of seeing the world. As though there would be results and things to count on as I made my way from one situation to the next. I was slowly learning that what was most real in my life had little to do with the world of appearances. It was much bigger than that, and indestructible. Like the moon in Hsu Yun's poem, I could smash it, ignore it, not even be aware of it, but it had its own purpose..

Slowly I learned to relax my grip and trust this mystery beyond my own intentions and capacities. This new trust was confirmed in meditation as I learned to melt into the silent power within, and it was confirmed in outer life, like when I ran into an old schoolmate on the day I was fired from my job, and was offered work at her couture handbag company. I felt I was being given help, and I was grateful.

Love still had its terrifying side – a deep sadness and longing – but I could no longer project these feelings on to Pearlie. Her sadness had been in some part my own, and in those months after she died I allowed it a place with me. Weakness and longing were as much a part of the inner Pearl as the light and love that grew brighter every day. There would be more crucifixions, there would be more loss, and there would be deeper and deeper realization of the wholeness running through all life. As God says in Corinthians: "My power is made perfect in weakness."[20] I knew this weakness would always be present, and perhaps in its depths His power would continue to grow.

Practicing Buddhism those years before, I learned of renouncing final liberation in order to remain in service in this world. And in Sufism there is a mysterious saying, "I want union with Him and He wants separation; thus I leave what I want so that His wish comes true."[21] I was beginning to understand that being alive would always be a sacrifice of some sort, and I tried to accept this sacrifice.

As I allowed both the beauties and pains of life, even the pain of my own failings, the peace that Pearlie first awakened me to grew stronger. Anxieties and concerns faded like so many other things, carried away by gentle waves of unknowing. I even gave up trying to understand the previous years on the path. I had the sense that my awareness would never offer a clear picture of anything, but instead would grow only in little pieces, always cycling back into a hidden place, like small flying fish breaking through the surface of the ocean catching the sun for only an instant before diving back into the darkness below.

And more and more I could follow those fish, diving with them back into the darkness, before rising again into the light of day.

Working with love had its own rewards. Pearlie had trained me in this work, showing me before she died how to follow love all the way into the densest parts of creation so even forgotten things could come alive. I practiced this all the time, and slowly watched how things changed when they were loved. And I saw how love could change even the most difficult situation. I learned this lesson during my first week in the handbag showroom, while I was packing boxes for shipment.

My second day packing boxes was the day that my teacher and all my old friends from our meditation group came to upstate New York for a week-long retreat. For five years I had organized and staffed that retreat for him. I had loved the experience, for I felt like I was helping him – I felt like I was special to him and part of his work. My position had also helped make the week especially intense, as I had to be attentive to the spiritual energy of the retreat, which was at times so powerful, while taking care of all the practical details. But I loved that challenge; I loved those summer weeks.

But this year I was, alone, in a strange showroom, packing thousand dollar handbags for Neiman Marcus, while my old friends and teacher were all together at a nearby retreat center meditating engaged with their spiritual work. Making matters worse was that no friend either flying into the city from Europe or from California had called to get together with me, even briefly, before or after the retreat, though most flew through New York, and knew I was there. I felt sad and alone, still unsure of what had caused this strange exile.

The first morning of the retreat, alone with my packing materials, I remembered where everyone was. The sadness came, and I tried to give it a place without letting it overwhelm me. I opened my heart to the extreme sorrow within, but I allowed my attention to stay where it was needed, on the handbags I was placing carefully in their boxes. Suddenly those bags seemed like precious children getting tucked into bed. I cared for them as though they were living beings. And soon into the morning there was just love. Love for what I was doing, love for God, love for my teacher. I did not feel left out, nor did I feel I was getting the short end of the stick. I was, instead, filled with the sense of blessing – a slight energetic gift of love and awareness that flowed through my consciousness and probably through my hands into all that leather and lizard skin, into each cardboard box. This love, while somehow part of me, was also so much more.

What a difference it is to help love flow where it is needed, rather than limit it to the object of one's desires This was the real gift of the last years – the taste of serving love. I could only hope that in the future, through the power and grace of my tradition, I would be given a way to live this state of being more completely.

The tree of life

I see, from way above, a vast desert of golden sand. I come closer, and the desert scene reveals some hills and valleys, undulating into eternity.

In the middle of my view is a huge, ancient tree, also gold in color, with large expansive branches and bright green leaves. There are so many people at the tree! My teacher is there, so is Pearlie, some old friends, and also people I do not know. The black seal, which kissed me on my left cheek in an earlier dream lies at the base of the tree – a glistening being of darkness against the dry, gold earth.

Now I am swinging from a long vine hanging off of a branch, swinging and swinging back and forth into the sky, filled with intense freedom and joy.

I remember doing my Buddhist practices of prostrations so long ago, which had included visualizing a "refuge tree" with the guru in the center of the tree and the teachers of the lineage rising upward from the center. The Buddhas and the Bodhisattvas are all present, as are the teachings of the Buddha, and relatives and other people surround the base of the tree. How strange to never have considered that this tree was the tree of life, that spiritual practice and devotion to the truth were all part of life.

What had I been doing all those years when I thought I was coming closer to the divine? I had no idea I had been avoiding the ground and the entryway to what is real. Now in this dream, I am shown how everything – my teacher, Pearlie, my friends, people I didn't know, the Seal of Communion who swam in the darkness and rose from those depths to claim me with her kiss – are all part of the tree of life. And I am here too, swinging from the tree back and forth, so far up into the empty sky, always connected to these people and to the earth below.

After prostrations, I had practiced creating a world of harmony and beauty and offering it and myself for the sake of the whole. That practice required sitting in my room in meditation with a bowl filled with beautiful jewels and nourishing grains of rice, spreading that mixture on a plate to create the image of world, then wiping it clean to start anew. My teacher had forced me to live this practice in life. These last years had been one sweep of the offering plate, but it seemed deep and true that I had lost an entire universe and also a small part of myself for the sake of something I could not understand.

It had been easier in my house alone with that rice! How much more difficult it was to really embrace and then lose the beauty and love that had nourished me those years on the path. To receive it in my own body, my own psyche, and to suffer its sacrifice. And I was sure this creation and loss would happen again and again, sweep after sweep, into greater perfection and greater emptiness, until a real detachment remained that connected me to everything.

And merging with the teacher – that final preparatory step that guides the disciple's absorption into the Real – this too could begin. The essential nothingness of my teacher could slowly seep into my being. I began to sense its haunting echoes and its intoxicating freedom in my daily life as much as in meditation.

It can still feel unnatural to me that life is the arena for spiritual devotion and practice, and some days I long to be back in a monastery. Moving through this world of choices and responsibilities with an expanding experience of emptiness is more difficult than sitting behind the walls of seclusion. Is this new, I wonder? Is it the need of this time? Are the doors to the monastery closed because life itself needs the love and awareness that had been directed somewhere else for so long? Or has it always been that life needs spiritual energy, and divine awareness expands itself outward through creation?

I can't pretend to know. But it has become clear that something that begins so far away beyond even the heart is needed in this world. Looking around, anyone can see that something is missing. Life can be reminded of its magical nature, the earth can be nourished by its own sacredness, and human beings can remember a deeper meaning of our existence.

According to the Naqshbandi Sufis, the Prophet declared: "I have two sides: one faces my Creator and one faces creation."[22] And the great Tibetan teacher, Tulku Urgyen advises the practitioner to "Upwardly generate devotion to all the enlightened ones, and downwardly cultivate compassion for all sentient beings."[23] I don't fear anymore that my commitment to one will cloud the other. And I long to learn more of how they are different and the same, how they are lived through a human being, and the new ways that the Creator can nourish His creation with our help. This longing is a deep and even physical hunger for more and more of what had been given with Pearlie's help, as though my being can be fed only on those mysteries.

With time, the confusion and pain around what happened between my teacher and me diminished, and a nearness is revealed. In one moment I knew he was in my heart. I felt us sitting up against each other, knee to knee, like two people on the floor of a dark and tiny closet, almost too close for my liking, as everything about me was utterly exposed to him. He knew every thought, every hope, every fear, and I would never be away from him.

In the months since the shock of losing him outwardly, his inner presence grew. How is he both completely present, and also becoming more so? It is indescribable. But I watch this miracle with gentle intensity, as though listening as footsteps approach through a hallway I feared had been closed forever. But here it is, open, lit with a devotion that would not fade. I don't know if I will see my teacher again for years, but this inner awareness matters more than I can say.

And Pearlie? There is a part of my heart that only she reminds me of. Some days I miss her. I look at her picture, hanging on my wall, running toward me with her big white eye, and some part of me wants to cry. I let myself cry occasionally, but other times I just remember her. Then we are together in all the simple glowing pearl that had been growing deep in the core of things.

Nothing else matters now. Everything of value spins from within that sacred space. If an inspiration, interest, or even a feeling does not resonate with this deeper knowing, does not find its rightful place at Pearlie's four little paws – well, it's just another nickel on the shrine, as my old friend Roger would say. Just another way to appease the gods and distract them from what they really want. Just another way to avoid the business at hand.

What is that business? I will probably never know. But it's some kind of funny business – some way to bring Pearlie more and more into life, so her big eyes, which still make me cry, can take in the world. And, of course, it is a way for the world to meet Pearlie, for who wouldn't benefit from a journey into her secrets, which are beginning to reveal themselves at every turn?

When, in a dream one night, I was told: "The 10 queens are waking up in the castle" I knew an inner darkness having to do with feminine consciousness and my relationship to life and had been transformed. Transformed by my growing love for Pearlie, from giving her a place in my heart. Pearlie the dark and rejected one had become 10 Queens in the castle of my soul – wisdom herself ten times over – revealing God in creation and the light of love within all life.

I remember that dream I'd had in which I was in a store selling old antiques. In a closet in the back of the store were two giant red apples, next to a tape of the Heart Sutra. I bit into one of those apples and I bought the belief that form and emptiness, life and death, here and there, were in essence one. That sweet juice that exploded in my mouth was like nothing I had ever experienced.

Will my new life be so sweet? The dove chicks hatching on the fire escape tell me so. And sometimes I can sense this sweetness in the night as flowers from a hidden garden send their fragrance through my window, and during the day when the sunlight from high windows flashes across the car tops and off the billboards and off the glasses of passersby, like a web of meteors.

And I know Pearlie would like this new life. I can see her now, running through the city when some people have gone to sleep and others are out on the town, her little paws padding through the glistening streets, sniffing out snacks at the back of restaurants, running in front of speeding taxis and stopping them in their tracks.

In this Big Apple of my heart I don't miss her so much, I just adore her – a glowing ball of white fur, an aurora borealis of softness streaking through the night, laughing, her big white eye demanding and crazy with visions of another world.

Endnotes

1   2 For more information, see *Torch of Certainty* by Jamgon Kongtrul, p. 10. Shambhala Publications, 1977.

3   *The Enlightened Mind*, Stephen Mitchell, p. 10. Harper Collins 1991.

4   *Love is a Stranger, Selected, Lyric Poetry of Jelaluddin Rumi*, translated by Kabir Helminski, p. 19. Shambhala, 2000.

5   See John 1.43, Mark 1.17, Matthew 9.9 and Matthew 16.24-25.

6   *Daughter of Fire*, Irina Tweedie, p. 169. Golden Sufi Center Publishing, 1995.

7   *Traveling the Path of Love, Sayings of the Sufi Masters* edited by Llewellyn Vaughan-Lee, p. 41. Golden Sufi Center publishing, 1995.

8   See www.goldensufi.org.

9   *Traveling the Path of Love*, edited by Llewellyn Vaughan-Lee, p. 94. The Golden Sufi Center, 1995.

10 Arabic version of Hermes' Emerald Tablet. See: http://www.sacred-texts.com/alc/emerald.htm

11 "Great Poems" by Hafiz from, *Drunk on the Wine of the Beloved*, translations by Thomas Rain Crowe, p. 58. Shambhala Publications, 2001.

12 *Dogs from a Sufi Point of View*, by Dr. Javad Nurbakhsh, p. 6. Khaniqahi-Nimatullahi Publications, 1989.

13 *The World of Myth*, David Adams Leeming, p. 36.

14 *Rumi: Poet and Mystic*, R. A. Nicholson, p.180. Unwin Hyman, 1978.

15 See chapter 6 "Women's Ways of Knowing, a Meeting With Sobonfu Some" from *The Unknown She*, Hilary Hart, p. 255. The Golden Sufi Center Publishing Co., 2003.

16 This excerpt from "The Heart of Transcendent Knowledge," more commonly known as "The Heart Sutra" from the Buddhist Mahayana tradition, was translated from the Tibetan with reference to the Sanskrit by the Nalanda Translation Committee under the direction of Chögyam Trungpa Rinpoche. Copyright 1975, 1980 by the Nalanda Translation Committee, 1619 Edward Street, Halifax, Nova Scotia B3H 3H9, and used with special permission.

17 John 14:27.

18 "A New Rule" from *Love is a Stranger, Selected Lyric Poetry of Jelaluddin Rumi*, translated by Kabir Helminski, p. 20. Shambhala Publications, 1993.

19 From "Separation and Union" by Llewellyn Vaughan-Lee, printed in issue 27 of Sufi: A Journal of Sufism, Khaniqahi Nimatullahi Publications.

20 Corinthians 12:9.

21 Al-Ghazzali, quoted by Llewellyn Vaughan Lee in *Love is a Fire*, p. 98. The Golden Sufi Center Publishing Co., 1995.

22 See www.naqshbandi.org, under Abdul Khaliq al-Ghujdawanai.

23 Tulku Urgyen Rinpoche, *Repeating the Words of the Buddha*, Rangjung Yeshe Publications, Kathmandu, 1991. p. 60.

Permissions

I extend my sincere gratitude to the following individuals and organizations for granting permission to use their work in this book.

Gorgias Press (www.gorgiaspress.com) for the use of an excerpt of William Wright's translation of "The Hymn of the Pearl."

Nalanda Translation Committee for use of their translation of "The Heart of Transcendent Knowledge," more commonly known as The Heart Sutra.

Zen Buddhist Order of Hsu Yun (www.hsuyun.org) for the use of Hsu Yun's poem "Strong Feelings Remembering the Way it Was When I First Started Out."

Daniel Ladinsky for the use of his translation of Hafiz's poem, "Where is the Door to the Tavern." From the Penguin publication, *The Gift, Poems by Hafiz*, copyright 1999 Daniel Ladinsky and used by his permission

The Golden Sufi Center for use of excerpts from *Daughter of Fire* by Irina Tweedie, *Love is a Fire* by Llewellyn Vaughan-Lee, and

Traveling the path of Love, edited by Llewellyn Vaughan-Lee, and for references to its website www.goldensufi.org.

Alireza Nurbakhsh for use of an excerpt from his father, Dr. Javad Nurbakhsh's book, *Dogs From a Sufi Point of View*, published by Khaniqahi-Nimatullahi Publications, 1998.

Efforts were made by the author to obtain permission for the use of all excerpted material.

Art credits

Author photograph by Jadina Lilien

Thanks to Roger and Cleary for photographs of Pearlie (Departure Day, Ears Like Wings).

All other Pearlie photographs by the author

About the author

Hilary Hart is author of *The Unknown She, Eight Faces of an Emerging Consciousness*, published by The Golden Sufi Center (www.goldensufi.org).

For more information about the author, please visit: www.hilaryhart.org.

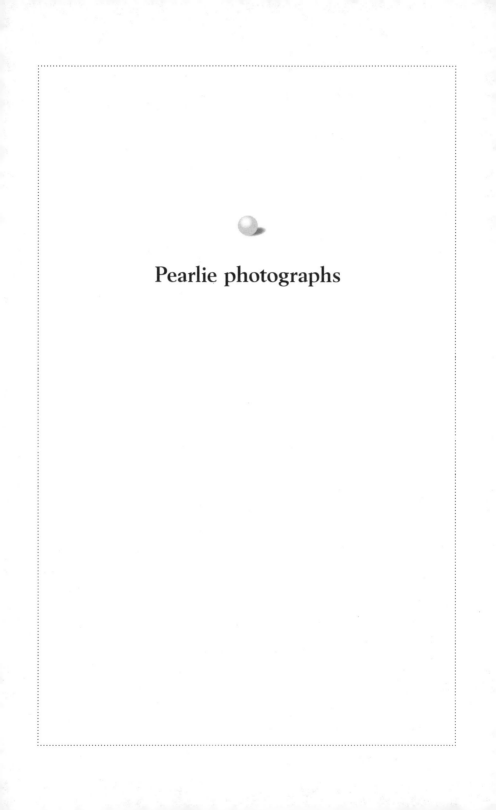

Pearlie photographs

Arriving in California

Ears like wings

On the run

Departure day

On the road

Near drowning

Pearlie in Connecticut

Happy to be here!

Heading home

Other O-books of interest

Created in the Image of God
A foundational course in the Kabbalah

ESTHER BEN-TOVIYA

This book provides a foundational course in the Kabbalah which speaks to the universal truths of the human experience, and is relevant to people of all backgrounds. It is a life changing, interactive course using the ancient tenets of the Kabbalah to pass on to you the experience of your unique place in the Eternal Worlds and to open your pathways of conscious conversation with the Higher Dimensions for everyday living.

9781846940071/1846940079•272pp £11.99 $21.95

Son of Karbala
The spiritual journey of an Iraqi

MUSLIM SHAYKH HAERI

A new dawn has appeared in spiritual travelogue with the publication of Son of Karbala. *It deserves a place among the great spiritual odysseys of our time, right next to Gurdjieff's* Meetings with Remarkable Men, *which it at once resembles and exceeds in its honesty and clarity.* – **Professor Bruce B. Lawrence**, Duke University, Durham NC

9781905047512/1905047517•240pp £14.99 $29.95

The Thoughtful Guide to Islam

SHAYKH HAERI

About as timely as any book can be, should be read, and re-read, not only by so-called Christians but by many Muslims too. – **The Guardian** *Thoughtful without being an academic textbook, Shaykh Haeri shows us the completeness of Islam and gives many insights. The scope of this Thoughtful Guide is impressive.* – **Sangha**

9781903816622/1903816629•176pp £7.99 $12.95

The Thoughtful Guide to Sufism

SHAYKH HAERI

A Sufi is a whole human being, primarily concerned with the "heart" that reflects the truth that exists within it beyond time and in time. The aim is to reach the pinnacle of "his" self by achieving physical silence. The Sufi path is one of self denial. I found this book an absorbing and heartfelt source of information.
– Sangha

9781903816639/1903816637•128pp £7.99 $14.95

You Called My Name

The hidden treasures of your Hebrew heritage

ESTHER BEN-TOVIYA

We are entering a new era of Jewish-Christian dialogue. This offers the reader a guided tour of Judaism, the religion of Jesus, that will enhance the spiritual lives of all who follow the religion about Jesus, Christianity. This is more than a book. It is a cherished resource. **– Rabbi Rami Shapiro**, author of *The Divine Feminine.*

9781905047796/1905047797•272pp £11.99 $19.95

1000 World Prayers

MARCUS BRAYBROOKE

This book is the most comprehensive selection of prayers from different traditions currently available. It is divided into five major sections: God (including silence, love, forgiveness), times and seasons, the changing scenes of life, the world and society, and the natural world. There is a contemporary as well as traditional flavour. **– Scientific and Medical Network Review**

9781903816172/1903816173•360pp•230x153mm £12.99 $19.95

Meditation: the 13 Pathways to Happiness

JIM RYAN

This book shows you how to meditate step by step, in an easy-to-follow and friendly guide. Each chapter is clarified and embellished by a meditation that enables the reader to reflect on and experience what has been said. Stories and quotes bring home it's relevance for millions of people from ancient times to the present. Used as a course by thousands around the world, these words are now published for the first time.

9781905047727/190504772X•128pp £9.99 $19.95

Peace Prayers from the World's Faiths

ROGER GRAINGER

Here eight different religions join together in peace to pray for peace, personal and global, under the auspices of the interfaith organization, The Week of Prayer for World Peace. This is a very practical prayer book, earthed in the pain of being human. It consists of seven weeks of prayer, each of which contains eight "days" of prayers and intercessions on particular themes connected with the overall theme of "Peace on earth and goodwill towards mankind".

9781905047666/1905047665•192pp £11.99 $21.95

O

is a symbol of the world,
of oneness and unity. O Books
explores the many paths of wholeness and spiritual understanding which
different traditions have developed down
the ages. It aims to bring this knowledge in
accessible form, to a general readership, pro-
viding practical spirituality to today's seekers.

For the full list of over 200 titles covering:
ACADEMIC/THEOLOGY • ANGELS • ASTROLOGY/
NUMEROLOGY • BIOGRAPHY/AUTOBIOGRAPHY
• BUDDHISM/ENLIGHTENMENT • BUSINESS/LEADERSHIP/
WISDOM • CELTIC/DRUID/PAGAN • CHANNELLING
• CHRISTIANITY; EARLY • CHRISTIANITY; TRADITIONAL
• CHRISTIANITY; PROGRESSIVE • CHRISTIANITY;
DEVOTIONAL • CHILDREN'S SPIRITUALITY • CHILDREN'S
BIBLE STORIES • CHILDREN'S BOARD/NOVELTY • CREATIVE
SPIRITUALITY • CURRENT AFFAIRS/RELIGIOUS • ECONOMY/
POLITICS/SUSTAINABILITY • ENVIRONMENT/EARTH
• FICTION • GODDESS/FEMININE • HEALTH/FITNESS
• HEALING/REIKI • HINDUISM/ADVAITA/VEDANTA
• HISTORY/ARCHAEOLOGY • HOLISTIC SPIRITUALITY
• INTERFAITH/ECUMENICAL • ISLAM/SUFISM
• JUDAISM/CHRISTIANITY • MEDITATION/PRAYER
• MYSTERY/PARANORMAL • MYSTICISM • MYTHS
• POETRY • RELATIONSHIPS/LOVE • RELIGION/
PHILOSOPHY • SCHOOL TITLES • SCIENCE/
RELIGION • SELF-HELP/PSYCHOLOGY
• SPIRITUAL SEARCH • WORLD
RELIGIONS/SCRIPTURES • YOGA

**Please visit our website,
www.O-books.net**